Stadium Stories:
Auburn Tigers

Stadium Stories™ Series

Stadium Stories:

Auburn Tigers

Phillip Marshall

INSIDERS' GUIDE®

GUILFORD, CONNECTICUT
AN IMPRINT OF THE GLOBE PEQUOT PRESS

INSIDERS' GUIDE ®

Copyright © 2005 by The Globe Pequot Press

Text design: Casey Shain
All photos courtesy Auburn Athletic Department except where noted.
Cover photos: *front cover:* Carnell Williams (Todd Van Emst); *back cover:* top, Shug Jordan; bottom, 1993 Auburn-Alabama scoreboard.

Library of Congress Cataloging-in-Publication Data

Marshall, Phillip.
    Stadium stories : Auburn Tigers / Phillip Marshall. — 1st ed.
      p. cm. — (Stadium stories series)
    ISBN: 0-7627-2311-4
    1. Auburn University—Football—History. 2. Auburn Tigers (Football team)—History. I. Title: Auburn Tigers. II. Title. III. Series.

GV958.A92M37 2003
796.332'63'0976155—dc22
                                         2005047643

Manufactured in the United States of America
First Edition/First Printing

Contents

The Early Years

George Petrie was an academic, a young history professor who had joined the faculty of the Agricultural and Mechanical College of Alabama in 1872. The college was renamed Alabama Polytechnic Institute in 1899, though the school was known colloquially as "Auburn." The school officially became Auburn University in 1960.

Petrie was a man of unquestioned integrity, but he was no shrinking violet. He believed in nourishing the physical as well as the mental. He loved sports. He was a bicyclist. He played tennis, golf, and baseball. Sometimes he would let his students out of class and join them for a game of kickball on campus.

Born in Montgomery, Alabama, Petrie showed an interest in scholarship from a young age. He went away to college and received two degrees from the University of Virginia before moving to Auburn. During his time at Auburn, he took a two-year leave to study for his doctorate at Johns Hopkins in Baltimore. When he returned with his degree in 1891 to join the Auburn faculty, he brought something else with him—a love for the game he'd seen for the first time. It was called football.

While at Johns Hopkins, Petrie met Charles Herty, a chemistry professor from the University of Georgia. Both men had taken great interest in the new game. They talked of forming teams at their respective schools and having them play against each other. Petrie returned to Auburn brimming with enthusiasm. He introduced the game to the students and faculty members. He recruited those who were interested, concentrating on the biggest and burliest, and put together a team. They practiced on the drill field behind Samford Hall. Petrie was both the coach and a player.

Georgia actually played a game before Auburn did, beating Mercer 50–0 on January 30, 1892. Not long after that, Petrie issued a challenge to his friend, Herty. It was readily accepted. Teams from Auburn and Georgia met in Atlanta for a game on February 20, 1892. Cliff Hare, whose name would later be emblazoned on Auburn's majestic football stadium, was a member of that first team. Later a long-time professor and dean of the school of chemistry, Hare went on to serve as chairman of the Auburn faculty athletic committee and president of the Southern Conference before the formation of the Southeastern Conference.

George Petrie, the academic who brought football to Auburn.

Hare's motto was "Athletics make men strong; Study makes men wise; Character makes men great." The Cliff Hare Award is given annually to the Auburn athlete who epitomizes these words.

The first Alabama-Georgia game was played at Piedmont Park in downtown Atlanta. Petrie borrowed the money to pay for his team's train trip to Atlanta. Dorsey and Culver scored touchdowns for Auburn, which counted 4 points each. Lupton added a goal, which counted 2 points, and Auburn won 10–0. In addition to Petrie, Dorsey, Culver, and Lupton, the team's roster included C. H. Barnwell, Richard B. Going, R. M. Stephens, H. H. Smith, H. T. DeBardeleben, H. R. McKissick, A. D. McLennan, W. E. Richards, A. W. Herren, S. J. Buckalew, F. M. Boykin, C. W. Dantzler, W. A. Culbreath, C. Y. McRee, Raleigh W. Green, D. E. Wilson, and J. Howard Smith.

It was a festive occasion. Thousands came to watch, some in carriages, some in buggies, some on horseback. The teams wore rugby caps and white jackets and trousers trimmed in the school colors. Georgia brought along a goat named Sir William as a mascot. A century later, in 1992, when Auburn and Georgia officials gathered at the site of the original game, Georgia's athletic director, Vince Dooley, paused to honor Sir William. "A billy goat might well have become Georgia's official mascot instead of a bulldog," Dooley said, "if shortly after the game, Sir William hadn't become barbecue."

Legend has it that Auburn's famed battle cry of "War Eagle!" originated that day in 1892. The story is this: A Confederate soldier named Eugene was lying near death on the battlefield. When he awoke, all he saw was a wounded baby eagle. The soldier was rescued and took the eagle with him and nursed him

Auburn's first football team poses for a photo in 1892.

back to health. Eugene eventually became a member of the Auburn faculty. When Auburn scored the first touchdown against Georgia, the old eagle broke free from its master and began to soar above the field. Auburn fans looked skyward, saw the eagle, and shouted "War Eagle!" The eagle collapsed and died, having given its all in pursuit of victory for Auburn.

It's a great story—it's just not true. The tale was actually written in 1959 by sophomore journalism student Jim Phillips in the *Auburn Plainsman*. Phillips, who later became one of the nation's top investigative reporters, never expected anyone to take it seriously. Nevertheless, even without the eagle, a tradition was born that winter day in 1892 in Atlanta. Except for the years 1917, 1918, and 1943, when war intervened, Auburn and Georgia have met annually in football. It is the oldest continuous series in the Deep South. Generations of young men have proudly represented their schools. They have played with uncommon ferocity and dedication and have written proud chapters in their schools' histories.

Petrie was revered by generations of Auburn students. Shortly after he retired in 1942, a group of student leaders asked if, based on his long service and experience at Auburn, he would compose a statement defining the principles that guide Auburn's academic community. In 1945, at seventy-nine, Petrie wrote the Auburn Creed. He died two years later. Today the creed is a cherished part of the fabric of Auburn University. It is read whenever the student body convenes and before athletic events. Auburn students and alumni know it by heart:

> I believe that this is a practical world and that I can count only on what I earn. Therefore, I believe in work, hard work. I believe in education, which gives me the knowledge to work wisely and trains my mind and my hands to work skillfully. I believe in honesty and truthfulness, without which I cannot win the respect and confidence of my fellow men. I believe in a sound mind, in a sound body and a spirit that is not afraid, and in clean sports that develop these qualities. I believe in obedience to law because it protects the rights of all. I believe in the human touch, which cultivates sympathy with my fellow men and mutual helpfulness and brings happiness for all. I believe in my country, because it is a land of freedom and because it is my own home, and that I can best serve that country

by doing justly, loving mercy, and walking humbly with my God. And because Auburn men and women believe in these things, I believe in Auburn and love it.

Nine months after beating Georgia in November 1892, Auburn played Duke, North Carolina, and Georgia Tech in a four-day span. The team that became known as the Tigers lost 34–6 to Duke and 64–0 to North Carolina before beating Georgia Tech 64–0. Earlier that month, on November 11, Alabama played its first game and beat a team of high school kids from the Birmingham Athletic Club 56–0. The next day, Birmingham beat Alabama 5–4. A month later, Alabama got revenge with a 14–0 win over the Athletic Club.

Even in those days, Auburn players were eager to get a shot at Alabama. They loved Petrie, but they wanted a coach from one of the schools "up East," where football had been played for several years, to get them ready. Auburn's manager wrote to F. M. Balliet, a former University of Pennsylvania center, and asked if he would coach the team. Balliet accepted. The eagerly anticipated game against Alabama was scheduled to be played at Lakeview Park in Birmingham on February 22, 1893. Auburn beat Alabama 33–22 that day. Auburn's manager could only thank Balliet for coaching the team—with many faculty members adamantly opposed to football, there was no money to pay him. Balliet understood, thanked the manager for the opportunity, and went home to Pennsylvania. G. H. Harvey coached the team to victories over Alabama and Vanderbilt in 1893. Balliet came back to help Harvey out again in 1893, and the team went 3–0–2. Coach F. M. Hall went 1–3 in 1894, but that one win was a 94–0 demolition of

Trouncing Tech

Auburn's third year of intercollegiate football was, for the most part, not memorable. It was the first season in which Auburn played an exclusively fall schedule and the first and only team coached by F. M. Hall. Auburn won just one of four games that season, falling 20–4 to Vanderbilt, 10–8 to Georgia, and 18–0 to Alabama. But on November 17 in Atlanta, the 1894 Auburn team made history, setting a record that still stands today and will probably stand for as long as the Tigers play football. The final score that day: Auburn 94, Georgia Tech 0. No Auburn team since has scored so many points in a single game.

In the first half, J. C. Dunham scored 2 touchdowns, one on a 60-yard run and one on a 15-yard run. Harry Smith, Charles Nelson, L. E. Bynum, J. V. Brown, and Walter Shafer also scored touchdowns. In the second half, Dunham ran 60 yards for a touchdown, Smith scored on runs of 64 and 25 yards, and R. G. Shanks on a 40-yard run. J. L. Glenn, Reynolds Tichenor, Walter Riggs, and F. D. Harvey also scored second-half touchdowns.

John Heisman took over as Auburn's coach in 1895, leaving Hall as a footnote in Auburn's football history.

Georgia Tech, still the most lopsided game in Auburn history.

John Heisman arrived in 1895, and Auburn football took a step toward becoming the dominant force in campus life that it is today. Years later, the most coveted award in college football would bear Heisman's name. Heisman had earned a law degree, but he went into coaching because he had an eye problem that made it difficult for him to read. Heisman was a Shakespearean actor in the off-season and a prolific writer. He used that creativity in talking to his players. Holding up a football at practice one day, he told them, "Better to have died as a small boy than to fumble this football."

In a game still in its infancy, Heisman was an innovator. The center snap, changing the common practice of rolling the ball to the quarterback, was his idea. He invented the hidden ball play in which the one player tucked the ball under the jersey of another. That innovation was soon outlawed, however. In five seasons at Auburn, Heisman was 12–4–1. He left for Clemson after the 1899 season. He went on to coach at Georgia Tech, Rice, Penn, Oberlin, Buchtel (now Akron), and Washington & Jefferson. He won 185 games and lost 70. He was at Georgia Tech when the Yellow Jackets beat Cumberland 222–0 in the most lopsided game in college football history. Heisman said he allowed the rout to show sportswriters the futility of using points as a basis to compare teams. But it wouldn't be a game or a career that would make Heisman famous. It would be a small, granite trophy.

Heisman was athletic director of New York's Downtown Athletic Club in 1935 when the club presented its first trophy to Chicago's Jay Berwanger as the nation's top college football player. Heisman was appalled. "How can you do that?" Heisman argued. "The best player? There is no such thing as the best player. They have to interact." But the trophy proved popular, and Heisman relented. He died the next year, and the trophy was named in his honor. Of all the schools at which Heisman coached, only Auburn has produced players who won the trophy that bears his name. Quarterback Pat Sullivan won it in 1971 and running back Bo Jackson in 1985.

John Heisman, for whom the Heisman Trophy was named.

After Heisman left, Billy Watkins, Robert Kent, and Billy Bates served short stints as Auburn's football coach. Mike Donahue arrived in 1904, and the first golden era of Auburn football was at hand. Donahue, who had to stretch to stand 5'4", had bright red hair and blue eyes. He looked like a professor, not a coach. He talked with a mixed Northern and Irish accent. Students at Auburn often couldn't understand what he said. Hundreds of Auburn students waited for the train carrying their new football coach. They were shocked when Donahue stepped out. "They were the most disgusted bunch of people I've ever seen," Donahue recalled years later.

Heisman had been immensely popular, but he'd not stayed long enough to establish Auburn as a power. Heisman got his first taste of fame at Georgia Tech. Donahue would make Auburn a name to be feared by opponents, a Southern powerhouse. When Donahue died in 1958, *Atlanta Journal* columnist Ed Danforth remembered how it had been: "You were nobody until you had beaten Auburn," he wrote. "That was the place card for the head table."

In the years between 1904 and 1922, Donahue was 99–35–5 at Auburn and won four Southern championships. For reasons lost in the passing of time, W. S. Keinholz was head coach in 1907 and Donahue was his assistant. Donahue took over again in 1908. Donahue coached Auburn to a 5–0 record in 1904 and quickly reached exalted status. But the Tigers were 2–4 in 1905 and 1–5–1 in 1906. Those lean years, perhaps, led to the new coaching arrangement in 1907. But from 1908 through the 1922 season, Donahue's teams only lost more than two games in a season twice.

Donahue's greatest days came in 1913–15. Starting with a 53–0 victory over Mercer in the 1913 season, the Tigers went twenty-three games without a loss, going 22–0–1. They outscored their opponents by the remarkable margin of 600–13. The 1913 team was named national champion by the Billingsley Report. Auburn, along with Harvard and Chicago, are listed by the NCAA as national champions for the 1913 season.

During its unbeaten streak, which would stand as Auburn's longest until Shug Jordan coached twenty-four games without a loss in 1956–58, the Tigers shut out twenty-one of the opponents. The 1914 Auburn team didn't give up a point all season but had to settle for a tie with Georgia. The streak finally ended with a 17–0 loss to Vanderbilt in Birmingham on November 13, 1915. On November 25, the Tigers lost 7–0 at Georgia Tech. Donahue suffered through a 2–5 season in 1918 but rebounded to go 8–1 in 1919, 7–2 in 1920, 5–3 in 1921, and 8–2 in 1922. In 1917 Donahue recorded what was then the biggest upset in Auburn history, even though it was a tie.

Southern football was considered inferior and was ridiculed in other parts of the country. When Auburn and Ohio State met in Montgomery on November 24, 1917, the undefeated Buckeyes were 30-point favorites. Auburn stopped Ohio State inside its 10 yard line five times, and the game ended in a scoreless tie. Even though it wasn't a win, it was further proof that Donahue had built a team at Auburn that could play with any in the country. The man who had disappointed students when he stepped off the train had become an Auburn hero. Donahue was far more than a football coach, however. He coached baseball, basketball, track, and soccer. He oversaw the mess hall. He taught classes in English, math, history, and Latin.

The more the football team won, the more popular the sport became on campus. No one seems to know just when it happened, but another tradition—victory celebrations at Toomer's Corner—

was born. Even before the turn of the century, Toomer's Corner was a gathering place. Before shopping malls and fast-food restaurants, it was the centerpiece of what students and townspeople called "Uptown." Want to go out for dinner? You went uptown. The Auburn Cafe, which later became the famed Auburn Grille, opened in 1902. In later years you could take in a movie at the Tiger or the War Eagle.

Toomer's Drug Store has been in business on the corner of College and Magnolia for more than a century. Sheldon Toomer, an entrepreneur and state senator in post–Civil War days, joined his stepfather, Benjamin Lazarus, in running the drug store after Toomer graduated from Auburn in 1893. Toomer later opened a hardware store nearby. As the years passed, politicians regularly stirred large crowds on Toomer's Corner with fiery speeches. Today, Toomer's Corner is known nationwide as the site of Auburn's victory celebrations. Students, senior citizens, and children fling rolls of toilet papers into the trees and even into cars. It is a cherished tradition that is uniquely Auburn. Parents bring their children as soon as they are old enough to walk. Freshman orientation includes a practice rolling at Toomer's Corner. A replica of Toomer's Corner was installed in the Lovelace Athletic Museum and Hall of Honor.

Donahue was fiercely competitive, but he believed football was a magnificent educational experience for the young men who played. He believed it so strongly that he once proposed that coaches be barred from the sideline during games. "My firm belief is that intercollegiate football will see a forward impulse toward a desirable goal when the coach is not permitted to sit on the sidelines," Donahue claimed. "What is the theoretical aim of competitive college sports? Why, the encouragement of resource and initiative among those who participate. How is the aim accomplished when the coach, from a vantage point on the sidelines, practically directs the play at important junctures, if not throughout? Personally, I had rather develop one man, a rounded man who can use his brains as well as his muscles, than a dozen All-American stars who have learned to depend upon the intellect of a non-participant." Donahue, no doubt, would have been shocked that, a century later, there would be specialists to coach every position and that Tommy Tuberville would sign a seven-year contract worth $18.2 million to coach Auburn's football team.

Donahue and his wife, Rosalie, had all five of their children while they lived in Auburn. Most thought he would retire there. But at the end of the 1922 season, LSU offered him $10,000 a year to change jobs. Donahue had become dissatisfied at Auburn, so he took the money and departed. When Donahue left, he didn't take his magic with him. He was never particularly successful at LSU. He was 23–19–3 in five seasons and then resigned. Donahue worked for a while as a club golf pro in Baton Rouge before becoming head football coach and athletic director at Spring Hill College in Mobile. He returned to LSU as director of intramurals in 1937. He retired in 1949 and lived in Baton Rouge until his death. He is a charter member of both the National Football Hall of Fame and the Alabama Sports Hall of Fame.

Once Donahue was gone, Auburn football struggled. Chet Wynne coached the Tigers to a 9–1 record in 1932, but his other three seasons were undistinguished. Jack Meagher took the Tigers to their first two bowls—the Bacardi Bowl in Havana, Cuba, on January 1, 1937, and the Orange Bowl, in Miami, on January 1, 1938.

The Phantom of Union Springs

Off the field Jimmy Hitchcock was soft-spoken and laid-back. Immensely popular among his teammates and classmates, he was a student leader at Auburn and later a leader in his community. He is remembered today by the Jimmy Hitchcock Award, given in Montgomery, Alabama, to the male and female high school athletes who display the greatest qualities of Christian leadership. On the football field, however, a change came over him. Instead of laid-back, he was aggressive and tough. It was there he earned his nickname, the "Phantom of Union Springs." As Billy Hitchcock, who followed his older brother to Auburn, recollected, "When he was on the field, he was one of the greatest competitors I've ever seen. He hated to lose. It was like his personality underwent a complete change. Once the game was over, he was back to being the kind of a slow-moving guy. But on the field, that was a different matter."

In 1932 Jimmy Hitchcock scored 71 points—spectacular for the day—as a single-wing tailback. He was a true triple threat—a runner, thrower, and punter. He led Auburn to a 9–0–1 record and the Southern Conference championship. Duke coach Wallace Wade called Hitchcock "the finest all-around back ever to play against any of my teams."

Under Carl Voyles and Earl Brown, Auburn went seven years without a winning record. After Brown went 0–10 in 1950, Shug Jordan returned to his alma mater in 1951 and began a journey to the 1957 national championship. Football was becoming a big business and the passion of millions of spectators. Neither Petrie nor Herty could have imagined such a thing when they organized the teams that started it all on a winter day at Piedmont Park.

Meagher's Marauders

The numbers alone aren't overwhelming. Jack Meagher won 48 games, lost 37, and tied 10 in his nine seasons as Auburn's head coach. He never won a championship, but the men who played for him bristle at the idea that Meagher was anything other than one of the great coaches and great men in the rich history of Southern football. They talk about him as a man who combined toughness and compassion, one who understood the game, and what it took to play it. As the years went by, they banded together and called themselves "Meagher's Marauders."

Nick Ardillo, a lifelong Birmingham educator who played his last season in 1941, credits Meagher as a major impact on his life and the lives of many of his teammates. "He was just a wonderful person" Ardillo recalls. "He was always very pleasant to be around. We all loved him. He was just a great fellow with a great sense of humor, and he stuck by his players. He never spoke a hard word to me the whole time I was there." In the 1980s Ardillo and others who had been touched by Meagher's brand of toughness and caring decided they should keep his memory alive. Meagher's Marauders were born.

The Marauders have disbanded now, but they decided in 2004 to sponsor an award to be given annually "to a person with Auburn affiliation who has made significant contributions to society through athletics." According to Ardillo, "It got down to where we were just a few and we were all too old to travel. We decided to disband, but we wanted to do something to keep the legend alive." The Marauders asked the Auburn Football Letterman's Club to pick the winner each year. Fittingly, the club chose the Marauders themselves as the first recipients of the award.

Billy Hitchcock was a two-way back in 1935–37 before going on to make his fortune as a Major League Baseball player, manager, and finally as a minor league executive. It was the day of leather helmets and players who never left the field. If you weren't a tough guy, you wouldn't last long. "We played great defense in those days," Hitchcock reminisces. "Coach Meagher made sure of it."

When Hitchcock was a senior in 1937, Auburn went to New Orleans to play Tulane. The game, rained out on Saturday,

Jack Meagher was beloved
by his players.

ended in a scoreless tie on Monday. Five days later, in Philadelphia, the Tigers played Villanova to a scoreless tie. "We had played two games in a week and nobody had scored yet," Hitchcock said. "That's the way the game was then." Auburn played hard-nosed, blood-and-guts football. It was the way Meagher had learned to play at Notre Dame. "We'd have maybe 40 points scored on us in a season, sometimes less than that," Hitchcock continued. "Coach Meagher was a great man for conditioning, too. After every practice, we'd run those 50-yard wind sprints. You'd run until you fell flat on your face." Sure enough, scoring on Auburn was an accomplishment in Meagher's days. When Hitchcock was a sophomore in 1935, the Tigers surrendered but 36 points in the 8–2 season. In 1936 they gave up 56 points, pitching 6 shutouts on the way to a 7–2 record. In 1937 they gave up 36 points, shutting out six opponents.

Auburn football had fallen on hard times when Meagher arrived in 1934. Chet Wynne had coached the Tigers to a 9–0–1 record and a Southern Conference championship in 1932, but that season had been an oasis in a football desert. Auburn had suffered through seven losing seasons in the eleven since Mike Donahue had left for LSU.

Meagher faced daunting challenges. Auburn Stadium wouldn't open until 1939. In Meagher's nine seasons, the Tigers played at home just eight times. Meagher didn't turn it around immediately, going 2–8 in 1934. But the Tigers were 8–2 in 1935. They were 7–2–2 in 1936, tying Villanova 7–7 in the Bacardi Bowl in Havana. It was Auburn's first bowl game and the only bowl ever played outside the United States. A year later, Auburn beat Michigan State 6–0 in the Orange Bowl.

After years of urging, Meagher finally got his stadium in his sixth season. There were concrete stands on the west side and wooden bleachers on the east. The grand old stadium celebrated its sixty-fifth birthday in 2004 with additional seats and luxury boxes that raised the capacity beyond 87,000. It is the sixth-largest on-campus stadium in the nation. More than seventeen million people have watched football games at this stadium.

On November 30, 1939, the Tigers played Florida to a 7–7 tie in the first game at Auburn Stadium, capacity 7,500. Babe McGehee scored the first touchdown on a pass from Dick McGowen. McGowen kicked the extra point. From that humble beginning, the stadium grew to seat 21,500. In 1949 the stadium was renamed Cliff Hare Stadium in honor of Clifford Leroy Hare, a member of Auburn's first football team, long-time president of the Southern Conference, and chairman of Auburn's faculty athletic committee. It became Jordan-Hare Stadium in 1973 in honor of Shug Jordan, who retired three years later after twenty-five seasons. The stadium has been enlarged nine times, but at its core, it is the same structure that was built two years before the start of World War II. "It's just a special place," says Kendall Simmons, an offensive lineman who finished his Auburn career in 2001 and plays now for the Pittsburgh Steelers. "It's the atmosphere. It's playing for Auburn. I never thought I would think so much of a place. I'm always going to come back here, regardless of where I am or what I'm doing." It is Meagher's legacy.

Like many other coaches of his day, Meagher was a Notre Dame product. He'd played two years for the Irish, earning respect as a tough-as-nails 155-pound end before joining the Marine Corps and going off to World War I. He returned to

Auburn Goes Bowling

Travel was nothing unusual for the Auburn Tigers of 1936. In Jack Meagher's third season, they had played in Detroit, at Santa Clara in San Francisco, Tulane in New Orleans, and Duke in Durham. They made all those trips by train. But after a 7-2-1 season, they were offered a trip that couldn't be made by train, at least not all of it.

Batista's Cuba was a freewheeling place in 1936. A national sports festival was planned, and a game of American football was to be the centerpiece. Auburn and Villanova were invited to participate. Auburn officials weren't so sure it was a good idea. Meagher was offered a $10,000 guarantee, but he wouldn't go until he had the money in hand. The money finally came, and Auburn set out for the first and only bowl game played in a foreign country. The team went by train to Tampa, then boarded a boat for Cuba. Famed Olympic sprinter Jesse Owens, who raced against a racehorse in the sports festival, was on the same boat. A disappointing crowd of 9,000 paid to watch the Bacardi Bowl in Havana on January 1, 1937. Most had no understanding of American football, but they cheered anyway. They were particularly excited when fights broke out on the field.

coach at little St. Edwards Institute in Austin, Texas. While he was coaching, he got his degree, graduating with honors. He moved to Rice, a Southwest Conference power, in 1929, and finally to Auburn. On November 21, 1942, Meagher coached

Billy Hitchcock scored on a 40-yard run for Auburn in the first quarter. Jimmy Fenton kicked the extra point. Villanova caught up by recovering a blocked kick in the end zone and kicking the extra point in the fourth quarter. That's how the game ended, in a 7–7 tie. The Auburn team returned from Havana via Miami. While in Miami, Meagher met the officials of another fledgling postseason game, the Orange Bowl. They wondered if Meagher would be interested in playing in the game when the conditions were right. Meagher said he would.

Auburn went 5-2-3 in 1937, but that was good enough for the Orange Bowl to extend an invitation for the Tigers to play Michigan State on January 1, 1937. Auburn won a bowl game for the first time, beating the Spartans 6–0 before a capacity crowd of 19,000 in a game that wasn't nearly as close as the score. The Tigers had 16 first downs to 2 for Michigan State, which had gone 8-1 in the Big Ten, then considered the nation's top conference.

George Kenmore returned a punt 60 yards to put Auburn in position for what was the game's only touchdown. Ralph O'Gwynne scored on a 2-yard run on fourth down in the second quarter, finishing off a 36-yard drive. Auburn's offense gained 312 yards to 57 for the Spartans. The victory provided a large dose of national publicity, but Auburn did not go to another bowl until the 1953 season.

Auburn to a victory that has stood the test of time, a 27–13 knockout of unbeaten Georgia that is still one of the bigger upsets in Southern football history and a grand moment in the South's grandest series.

The guns of World War II were growing louder when Meagher went with his team for what surely was a lost cause. In nearby Phoenix City, Alabama, bookies were giving four-to-five touchdowns to anyone foolhardy enough to put money on the Tigers. Georgia had Frank Sinkwich and Charlie Trippi and was on its way to the Rose Bowl. Football had been a lot of fun at Georgia in 1942. The Bulldogs rolled into Columbus unbeaten. They'd beaten Florida 72–0, the same Florida team that had beaten Auburn 6–0. Auburn had won four, lost four, and tied one. But Meagher's men believed. They believed in their coach and in themselves. They believed they could bring down this college football giant. Meagher had a plan for Georgia, and his players made it work. The stunned Bulldogs who, anticipating a rout, had no answer. The game really wasn't as close as the score would suggest; Auburn clearly out-played Georgia.

Auburn ran from the T-formation for the first time, catching Georgia by surprise. Meagher also unveiled a new defensive plan. Tackles would drop back, covering for rushing ends. Fifty years later, a similar scheme became popularly known as the zone blitz. Georgia scored first when Sinkwich went over from the 2 yard line, and it seemed this game would go as expected. But Auburn halfback Monk Gafford and his teammates, most of whom would be soldiers a year later, had other ideas. Not only did the Tigers beat Georgia's greatest team, they dominated. All through the long afternoon, they threatened to blow it open and make an embarrassing Georgia day even more embarrassing.

Gafford, a senior, became in 1942 the first Auburn runner to break 1,000 yards. He was a bona fide All-American who earned fame nationwide. But he never did get comfortable talking about

Jack Meagher, behind center, at practice.

his exploits. "I'd say I had some sort of complex about the publicity I got," Gafford admitted. "My teammates had as much to do with me making it as I did. I felt like they should have gotten part of it. It takes eleven people to play the game." But Gafford took great pride in the day Georgia fell. Georgia's Frank Sinkwich recalled years later, "I remember we beat Florida 75–0 and Florida beat Auburn 6–0. We thought we would win." Gafford and his teammates saw it differently. "We felt like we should have beaten them the year before," he said. "In 1942, everyone wanted to prove we should have. We were outweighed by 20–25 pounds per game, but when eleven people make up their minds at once, they are hard to beat." As time ran out and his players celebrated around him, Meagher shed tears of pride and joy. Auburn fans roared in celebration at Memorial Stadium in Columbus, Georgia.

A year earlier Georgia had won 7–0 on a late touchdown. Meagher was still rankled by that as the 1942 season neared. Johnny Meagher, the coach's teenage son, wondered if his father was getting a little carried away when he told him the Tigers would win. "Daddy told me that summer he was going to beat Georgia," recalls Johnny Meagher, retired now and living in Auburn. "Reading the papers about how good Georgia was, I was a little nervous." Johnny sold programs that day as the crowd streamed into the stadium. The game had already started when he took his place on the sideline. "When I got down there, Georgia had the ball and Sinkwich was running all over the place. They went down and scored. It didn't look good, but after that, it was all Auburn. My daddy knew what he was talking about when he said Auburn was going to win."

After Georgia took a 6–0 lead, Gafford's 34-yard run was the key play on Auburn's first scoring drive. Auburn got the ball back and went marching again. Jimmy Reynolds scored on a 4-yard run. Zach Jenkins had runs of 22 and 14 yards, setting up Gafford's 3-yard touchdown run on fourth down. Astonishingly, Auburn led 14–6, but surely the Bulldogs would pull themselves together. They tried, but the upstart Tigers wouldn't let it happen. Reynolds scored again from close in and it was 20–6, but Georgia wasn't done yet. Sinkwich threw a touchdown pass to Racehorse Davis to make it 20–13. Georgia's hopes died when the Tiger defense knocked the ball loose from Sinkwich, and Fagan Canzoneri recovered in the end zone for the final Auburn touchdown. Auburn fans celebrated long into the night. Georgia went home stunned, but the Bulldogs would show just how significant Auburn's victory had been by routing Georgia Tech 34–0 in its reg-

Meagher's Last Stand

The 1942 Auburn football season would scarcely be remembered at all had it not been for a stunning 27–13 victory over number-one-ranked Georgia on November 21. But, though no one knew it at the time, the Bulldogs caught an Auburn team hitting its stride. The Tigers had beaten LSU 25–7 a week earlier and routed Clemson 41–13 a week after Georgia. With World War II going full-bore, there were more important things than football in 1942. A year later, the coaches and players were off fighting for their country, and Auburn would have no football team.

ular season finale and shutting out UCLA 9–0 in the Rose Bowl.

With war raging in Europe and in the Pacific, Auburn did not play football in 1943. Meagher joined the navy. For Meagher and for most of those who played, fighting for their country was the natural and right thing to do. Football would have to wait. It was widely assumed that Meagher would return after the war, but it wasn't to be.

"He was something special," Hitchcock reminisces. "He was a tough little guy, and he was smart. Outside, he had a very calm demeanor. I never once heard him raise his voice. He'd say, 'All right, boys, let's go, let's go.' He had toughness inside." Though Meagher's players loved him and knew they received love in return, they learned quickly there were limits to his patience.

Those who didn't want to work didn't last. Center Jimmy Fenton was a talented football player, but early in his career he wasn't displaying the intensity Meagher wanted to see. According to Hitchcock, "He was a little bit lackadaisical, a little bit lazy. Coach Meagher ran him off." Fenton learned his lesson and returned to letter in 1935–37. Meagher would later say that Fenton was one of his all-time favorite players.

Johnny Meagher still lives in the house Jack and Francis Meagher built in 1939 on Wright's Mill Road in Auburn. He remembers his father as loving yet demanding, caring but unbending in standing for what he believed. "He was a pretty strict disciplinarian. He wanted you to stand up and do the right thing. I guess that just came to him naturally." Johnny was in the first grade when his father signed a three-year contract to coach football at Auburn. He remembers the excitement when they arrived, the anticipation of a new day for Auburn football. "I remember going down to old Alumni Gymnasium. They had an A-Club room down there with old pictures and stuff. I remember seeing something about Mike Donahue. I felt like that was before the beginning of time, almost. It had only been eleven years."

Jack Meagher never returned to Auburn to work. When the war was over, he went to coach the professional Miami Seahawks. One of his assistants was former Auburn player Shug Jordan, who had been freshman coach on his Auburn staff. When Earl Brown was fired after the 1950 season, Auburn's search committee contacted Meagher to see if he'd be interested in returning. He wasn't, but he recommended Jordan. Jeff Beard, the new athletics director, already knew he wanted Jordan.

Auburn was soon enjoying the greatest days in its history. Johnny's brother, Pat, played halfback on Jordan's 1957 national championship team.

Meagher died in 1968 (Francis Meagher lived in the house on Wright's Mill Road until 1997), sixteen years before he was inducted into the Alabama Sports Hall of Fame. He left a legacy of respect and love for those who played for him. Time has not dimmed their memories of those days long ago, when the helmets were made of leather and a coach with velvet in his voice inspired young men to great things. "We probably weren't very talented," Hitchcock muses. "We probably weren't as talented as a lot of teams we beat, but Coach Meagher made us believe we could do just about anything. And a lot of times, we just about could."

Together Again

They saw the smirks and heard the taunts. They saw wads of dollar bills waved in their faces, money the crimson-clad fans had bet that Auburn couldn't even stay on the field with Alabama. That's how it was on December 3, 1949, as Auburn football players left their hotel in Roebuck on the east side of Birmingham for the bus ride to Legion Field. In most courts, there wasn't any debate about who would win. It was only a question of just how bad it might be. And there was reason to believe it could be bad. When the Tigers and Tide had gotten together the previous season for the first time since 1907, it had not been pretty for anyone of an Auburn persuasion. Alabama had gone to Legion Field to make a statement and had made it loudly and clearly with a 55–0 victory.

Even then, long before the game came to be called the Iron Bowl and was one of the nation's top rivalries, Auburn people fought for respect in their own state. But this game really wasn't the biggest for either team. Auburn's big rivals were Georgia Tech and Georgia. Alabama's were Tennessee and Georgia Tech. This game was big only because the two teams shared the same state and because the state legislature had to get involved in making them play after they had ignored one another in football for more than four decades.

But on a crisp, autumnlike day four years after the end of World War II, a rivalry was born, one that would become as fierce as any in college football. Alabama went to the game favored by 3 touchdowns. The Tide had some of the South's top players, men like Eddie Salem, Butch Avinger, Red Lutz, Al Lary, and Herb Hannah. As was often the case with Red Drew's teams, this one picked up speed as November arrived. The Tide had lost early games to Tulane and Vanderbilt and had tied Tennessee. But then came consecutive wins over Georgia, Georgia Tech, Southern Mississippi, and Florida. All was right in the Alabama world.

Earl Brown was in his second season at Auburn. He never accomplished much on the field and was fired a year later after an 0–10 season in 1950. But for one day, Brown was a hero. The Tigers brought the likes of Johnny Wallis, Travis Tidwell, Tom

Earl Brown was coach when Auburn beat Alabama on December 3, 1949.

Banks, Billy Tucker, Jim McGowen, Ralph Pyburn, Erk Russell, and Bill Davis to Birmingham. They weren't as well known as some who played for Alabama. They had won just one game, Mississippi State, and had tied Florida, Georgia, and Clemson. Ole Miss, Georgia Tech, Tulane, and Vanderbilt were too much for the Tigers to handle.

Tidwell, who some will tell you to this day was as good as any player who has ever worn Auburn blue, was a quarterback who could run and throw. Three years earlier, he'd led the nation in total offense as a freshman. But the game that endeared Tidwell forever to Auburn people was his last one. He led Auburn to a 14–13 victory over Alabama, a win that echoes still through the years. For Tidwell it was redemption. The year before, he'd suffered an ankle injury in the second quarter and had listened from a hospital bed as Alabama poured it on. "Everybody will remember that, mostly Auburn folks," Tidwell said not long before he died in 2004. "We went in decided underdogs. Beating them 14–13 was harder for them to take than if we'd beaten them 40–0. That made me enjoy it that much more." It was a bruising game, what people today would call a "smashmouth" game.

Alabama started from its 13 yard line early in the second quarter and quickly found trouble. From the 16, Salem threw a pass for Lary. The ball never got there. Wallis cut in front and fled 18 yards for Auburn's first touchdown against Alabama since 1906. Billy Tucker kicked it to 7–0. The crowd was stunned, but a betting man who had put his money down on Auburn still would have had good odds. Order seemed to have been restored when Salem ran 13 yards for a touchdown and kicked the extra point. It was 7–7 at halftime, surely just a matter of time until the Tide took over.

After Brownie Flournoy intercepted a Salem pass at his 29 late in the third quarter, Auburn geared up for the drive that eventually made the difference. Bill Davis took it home from the 11 and Tucker kicked. It was 14–7, and the Auburn fans on the west side were getting louder by the moment. As the clock melted away, Alabama mounted one last charge from its 47 yard line. There was no two-point conversion in those days, and no one had ever thought of overtime. The best Alabama could do was a tie, but by this time that would not have been as embarrassing as a loss.

Calvin crashed into the end zone from the 1 yard line. All that was needed was a Salem kick, and Alabama would avoid humiliation. Auburn would be left with its fourth tie. But Salem's kick sailed wide to the right, setting off a wild scene in the west stands. Auburn recovered the ensuing onsides kick, and Tidwell ran out the clock. Auburn fans celebrated deep into the night.

When it was over, Auburn players didn't go for their coach. They went for Tidwell, hoisting him on their shoulders and carrying him off the field in celebration. For Russell, a two-way end who had dreamed of playing at Alabama only to snub the Tide at the last minute, it was a glorious finish to a tough career: "There were some lean, lean years in there, but what a great way to finish up. That was a great experience."

Tidwell had signed with Auburn to play for Coach Carl Voyles. After two seasons, Voyles had left and been replaced by Brown, a Notre Dame man. "Coach Voyles was a hard-nosed guy," Tidwell remembers. "We would scrimmage until dark and after. It didn't matter how tired we were. We kept going. They didn't let you have any water in those days, either. He believed in blood-and-guts football. He was a great coach, but the alumni and news media didn't like him and he didn't care. Earl Brown had on a bow tie and brown suede shoes just about every time I ever saw him. He had a great personality and could get along with the alumni and the reporters pretty well. He was a good guy, but the problem was he couldn't coach at all."

It was just more than a year after Brown's biggest victory that Shug Jordan became Auburn's coach. Instead of underdogs, the Tigers were favorites. Big wins were expected. They won a national championship. As the years went by, the game Jordan later dubbed the Iron Bowl became the defining moment in every season, bigger than Georgia, bigger than Georgia Tech, bigger than Tennessee, bigger than any of them. Generations of little boys grew up playing football in their backyards, pretending to be heroes from one school or the other, leading their team to a great victory. The lucky ones had the chance to experience it in real life. It became, by most estimations, the fiercest rivalry in college football, one in which players found something inside themselves to go beyond the ordinary and accomplish great feats. The good plays and the bad, the blowouts and the nail-biters, all became part of the state's football lore. The stories are told and retold through the generations. Even players who come from other states soon are swept up in the drama and emotion of Iron Bowl day.

"That game changes you forever," remembers Ben Leard, who came from Hartwell, Georgia, to be an All-Southeastern Conference Auburn quarterback. "Nothing compares to it. It is the epitome of intensity. Every backyard football game, every high school game you've ever played, every workout you've ever

Bo Over the Top

It had been ten long, hard years for Auburn's football faithful. Since an historic 17–16 victory in 1972, the Tigers had not beaten Alabama. Most of the games had not been close.

Though the Tigers were 7–3 and bound for the Tangerine Bowl, head coach Pat Dye's second Auburn team went to Birmingham's Legion Field an underdog again on November 27, 1982. Little did the Tigers know that Alabama coach Bear Bryant would announce his retirement weeks later. Alabama dominated most of the game, but Auburn stayed close. In the fourth quarter, which the Crimson Tide proudly proclaimed its own, Auburn shook off a decade of frustration. Alabama led 22–14 going into the fourth quarter, but freshman sensation Bo Jackson broke loose on a long run to set up a 23-yard Al Del Greco field goal that cut it to 22–17.

Down to their last chance, the Tigers started from their own 34 yard line. An Alabama interception was wiped out by an interference penalty. Finally, it was fourth-and-goal at the 1. The call went to Jackson, who went high over the line. He collided with the middle of the Alabama defense, but a final lunge got him into the end zone. A two-point conversion failed, but Alabama couldn't answer and the celebration began.

Auburn fans stormed the field and tore down the goal posts. Auburn coaches and players returned to join the celebration. The yoke of domination had been thrown off.

had, leads to that game. It's the pinnacle of football to be involved in it. There's always a hero on one sideline or the other you wouldn't think would do it. Guys suddenly step to the top and are heroes in this game. And they'll remember it forever."

Long after they are gone, Bill Newton and David Langner will be remembered for what happened on December 2, 1972. Newton blocked 2 punts, and Langner ran them both in for touchdowns as Auburn stunned unbeaten Alabama 17–16. But their story is only one of many. The 1989 Tigers will be remembered as the team that won 30–20 when Alabama finally played at Jordan-Hare Stadium for the first time.

Mailon Kent has been extraordinarily successful in business and in life, but he is most remembered for a day more than forty years ago. After being Auburn's starting quarterback in 1962, Kent had sustained a partially torn medial collateral ligament shortly before the 1963 season. Given the opportunity, Jimmy Sidle took over and was on his way to an All-America season by the time Kent was healthy. Sidle remains to this day the only quarterback in Southeastern Conference history to rush for more than 1,000 yards in a season. Kent, a senior, had played a few snaps against Florida State and a few snaps against Georgia as Auburn confounded the experts by winning eight of its first nine games. As the annual game against Alabama, also 8–1, neared, the talk was of a duel between Sidle and Alabama's Joe Namath. Kent was but an afterthought.

It's a quarterback cliché that the backup is only one play from being thrust into the spotlight, but it was more than a cliché for Kent on November 30, 1963. Paul Bryant was in his sixth season as Alabama's head coach, and Auburn had come under his spell. The Tide had shut out Auburn in four straight seasons, winning 10–0, 3–0, 34–0, and 38–0. Although Kent completed just two passes that cold, raw day against Alabama, they would be the two biggest passes of his career. "On second down, we had the wind and the ball about midfield," Kent remembers. "Eddie Vesperille hit Jimmy and about three or four of them fell on top of him. They knocked the breath out of him."

Offensive coordinator Buck Bradberry turned to Kent and told him to go into the game and keep the offense moving. "It was freezing cold and I hadn't even warmed up," Kent says. No problem. Kent threw a 12-yard pass to Bucky Waid for a first down. That set up Woody Woodall's 32-yard field goal, which gave Auburn its first points and first lead against Alabama since 1958. Sidle returned, but when Auburn faced third-and-goal at the Alabama 8 in the third quarter, Kent got the call again. He hit Tucker Frederickson for a touchdown and Auburn won 10–8. It was another Iron Bowl story for the ages. Time has marched on, but the feats of Iron Bowl heroes still echo.

Who could forget:

- Lloyd Nix, Tommy Lorino, Jackie Burkett, Zeke Smith, Red Phillips, Jerry Wilson, and friends leading the Tigers to a 40–0 rout that locked up the national championship in 1957

- Connie Frederick running 82 yards on a fake punt as the Tigers broke a five-game losing streak in the series 49–26 in 1969

- Pat Sullivan and Terry Beasley leading a rally from a 17–0 deficit to a 33–28 victory in 1970

- Newton and Langner's version of Instant Replay in 1972

- Bo Jackson going over the top for the winning touchdown on one of the more famous plays in Auburn history as the Tigers ended ten years of frustration 23–22 in 1982. Fans stormed the field and tore down the goal posts when it was over.

- Jackson assaulting the Tide defense for 256 yards in a 23–20 Auburn victory in 1983

- Lawyer Tillman's run to glory on a reverse as Auburn won 21–17 in 1986

- Patrick Nix's touchdown pass to Frank Sanders, which turned the game as Auburn finished a perfect season with a 22–14 victory in 1993

- Jaret Holmes's game-winning field goal that put the Tigers in the SEC Championship Game in 1997 with an 18–17 victory

- The heroics of reserve tailback Tre Smith as Auburn won 17–7 in Tuscaloosa in 2000

- Carnell Williams's 80-yard sprint on the first play from scrimmage as Auburn won 28–23 in 2003

- The icy determination of quarterback Jason Campbell as Auburn finished a perfect regular season with a 21–13 victory in 2004

It's difficult to comprehend that, for forty-one years, the Tide and Tigers did not play each other at all. Though legend has it that the series was discontinued because of a fight, it wasn't that way at all. Auburn wanted expenses of $3.50 per day for twenty-two players, but Alabama only offered $3.00 per day for twenty players. Auburn coach Mike Donahue wanted a Northerner to officiate the game; Alabama wanted a Southerner. That dispute turned into a football separation that lasted more than four decades.

Billy Hitchcock, who lettered from 1935–37, never played against Alabama in football. Players on both sides wondered why. "We wondered about it, too," Hitchcock recalled. "We were friends with them. In summer baseball, we played in the amateur

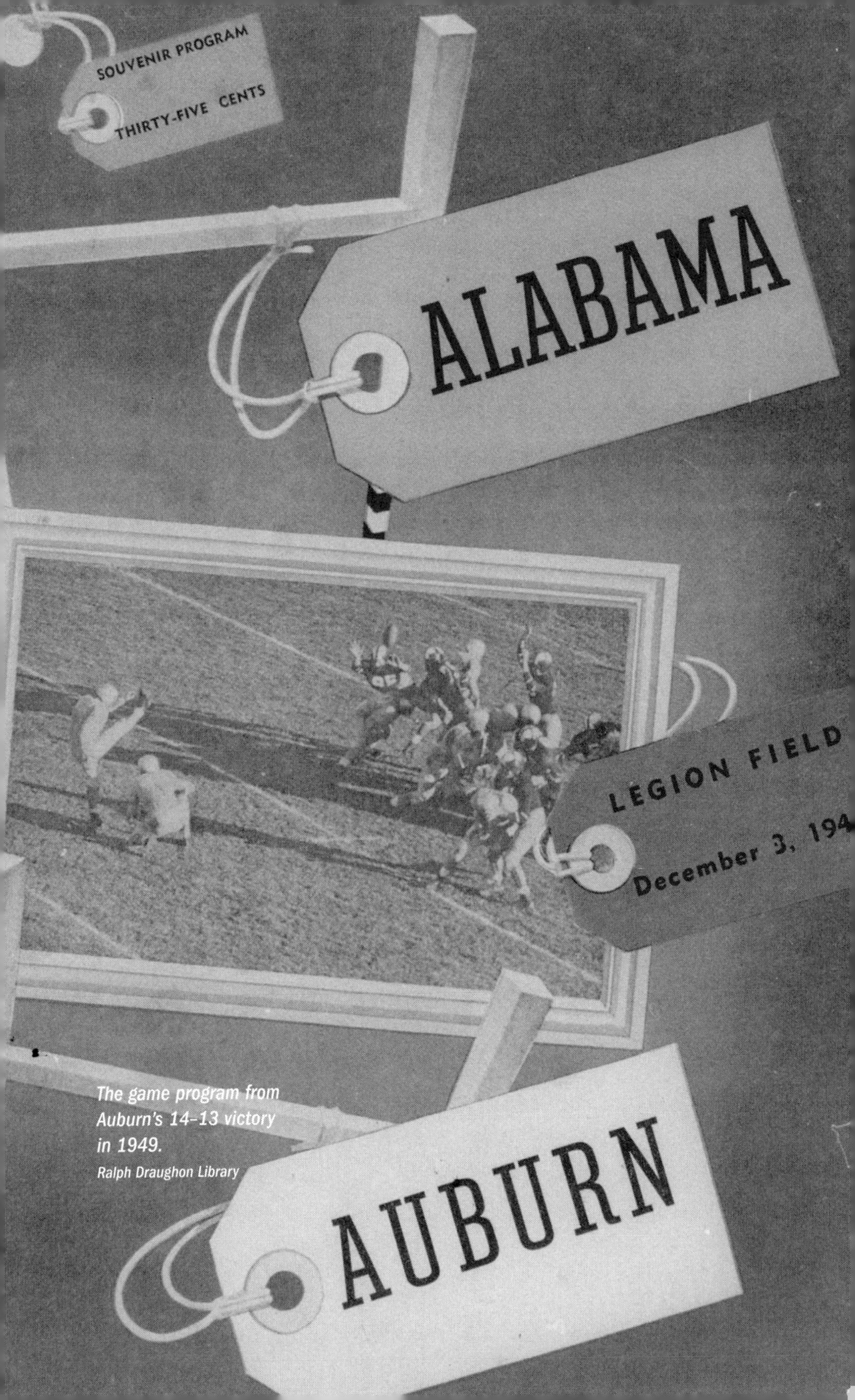

SOUVENIR PROGRAM
THIRTY-FIVE CENTS
ALABAMA
LEGION FIELD
December 3, 194
AUBURN

The game program from Auburn's 14–13 victory in 1949.
Ralph Draughon Library

league with Alabama players. We didn't know why we weren't playing. We all wanted to play. It took a long time, but they finally got around to it. The story we always heard was that they were afraid there would be a fight on the field. As far as I know, there's never been a serious incident on the field. It's the fans in the stands that cause the problem."

In 1947 the Alabama House of Representatives passed a resolution urging the schools to "make possible the inauguration of a full athletic program between the two schools." Finally, on December 4, 1948, Auburn and Alabama met again at Legion Field. It was no contest. But Tidwell led the Auburn upset a year later, and the seeds of what would become an historic rivalry were planted.

Alabama, which leads the all-time series 38–29–1, won the next four, but Auburn was closing fast under Jordan. The Tigers won 28–0 in 1954 and were off on a five-game winning streak in the series. Bear Bryant arrived at Alabama in 1958 and won nineteen of the next twenty-five games. Since Auburn broke through in 1982, the series has been remarkably close. Auburn has won thirteen and Alabama eleven.

Auburn coach Tommy Tuberville had heard stories of the Iron Bowl before he arrived in late 1998. Experiencing it, he said, is an opportunity to be cherished for a player or a coach. "It's unlike any other game," Tuberville reflects. "You can feel it the week before the game. You can see on the practice field that it's different for the kids. The atmosphere at the game is different than any other. It's a lifelong dream for a lot of these kids, especially the ones who grew up in Alabama, to make a difference in that game."

Dameyune Craig was one of those Alabama kids. He experienced the entire range of Iron Bowl emotions in his two seasons as starting quarterback. He saw Alabama rally in 1996 for a 24–23 victory at Legion Field. And he helped Auburn rally for an 18–17 victory at Jordan-Hare Stadium a year later. "I wish everybody could just line up one time and walk the Tiger Walk and walk on that field in uniform," Craig exclaims. "That's the best feeling I think any young man from Alabama can experience. I wasn't even mad when I wasn't playing. I was just happy to be on the field and be part of it."

Those childhood dreams also came true for tailback Carnell Williams in 2003. Controversy was swirling. Word on the street was that Tuberville was coaching his last game at Auburn. Players ignored the talk and went about their business. On the first play from scrimmage, offensive coordinator Hugh Nall planned a run with a blocking scheme Alabama's defense had not seen. Williams, Auburn's star tailback who had grown up an Alabama fan but had chosen Auburn in a bitter recruiting battle, got the call. It worked even better than Nall imagined. Williams, sweeping to his right, turned up field and was gone, 80 yards for the biggest touchdown of his life. The noise from the capacity Jordan-Hare Stadium crowd echoed inside his helmet. "As soon as I got it and I broke out, they kind of took a bad angle and I cut out," Williams recollects. "I didn't see anything but green grass. I said 'Man, I think I'm about to go the distance.' Growing up in this state, watching that game, watching Bo break long runs, watching other guys do their stuff, to do that on the first play was the greatest feeling ever."

For Williams, it was even more special because of the events of the previous two seasons. As a freshman, Williams had been off to a fast start against Alabama only to suffer a broken collarbone. He

Terrific in T-Town

Toilet paper, glistening white in the sun, hung from the trees on Toomer's Corner on Sunday morning, November 24, 2002. At Tiger Rags bookstore, the hot-selling item was a T-shirt that read: ALOHA, BAMA. 17–7. FROM THE SCHOOL DOWN THE ROAD.

The day after Auburn's football team earned a victory over number-nine Alabama at Bryant-Denny Stadium, coach Tommy Tuberville declared that his players "were bound and determined they weren't going to let anything stand in the way of winning that game." Students and townspeople stormed Toomer's Corner, the traditional site of Auburn victory celebrations, within minutes of the final horn. While Auburn players celebrated with the 10,000 or so who had made the trip to Tuscaloosa, toilet paper filled the air back home.

Labeled "The School Down the Road" by Alabama coach Dennis Franchione in his determination to avoid saying the word *Auburn*, the Tigers went on the road as underdogs and returned home as con-

had to watch from the sideline as the Tide romped 31–7. As a sophomore he'd suffered a broken leg against Florida. He could do nothing but provide moral support for Smith on the sideline as the Tigers earned some revenge with a 17–7 victory in Tuscaloosa. "Since I was knee-high as a kid watching the Iron Bowl, all those great games, I always wanted to play in it," Williams says. "It was just as great as I imagined it to be. The intensity level is so high. Everybody wants to win. You don't even want to think about not winning that game. It means so much to so many people. The atmosphere querors. They finished their regular season at 8–4 and 5–3 in the Southeastern Conference, earned a bid to play Penn State in the Capital One Bowl, and sent Alabama (9–3 and 6–2) reeling toward Saturday's game at Hawaii.

With freshman Tre Smith, who was fourth team at midseason, starting at tailback and tight end Cooper Wallace starting at fullback for the injury-riddled Tigers, few gave Auburn a real chance to win. But with Smith, quarterback Jason Campbell, and tight end Robert Johnson leading the makeshift offense, the Tigers grabbed a 17–0 halftime lead. The defense never let Alabama's offense get in sync and took it home from there.

The loss made Alabama's all-time record 0–4 against Auburn in Tuscaloosa an embarrassing number that increased to 0–5 two years later. It was sweet revenge for Auburn, which had been favored a year earlier at Jordan-Hare Stadium, only to be embarrassed 31–7 by the Crimson Tide.

is different than any other game. Tiger Walk is unbelievable. You can look in people's faces and see how much it means to them. You want to go out and play hard and win for your teammates, for your coaches, for yourself, and for all the Auburn people."

The Iron Bowl of today is a fixture on national television. It has been the subject of books and documentaries. A state comes to a stop on the day it is played. But it was that unlikely Auburn victory of long ago that made a game a rivalry and changed the course of a state's football history.

Shug and Jeff

Shug Jordan and Jeff Beard, the football coach and the businessman, are forever linked at the very heart of the thriving enterprise that is modern-day Auburn University athletics. In 1950 Auburn's football program was at an all-time low. Three years under Earl Brown had produced records of 1–8–1, 2–4–3, and 0–10. His only significant victory came in 1949, a 14–13 win over Alabama. And, as is the case today, if all wasn't well with the football program, all wasn't well with the athletic program as a whole. Auburn president Ralph Draughon loved football. He went to Jeff Beard, who was the business manager for Auburn's athletic program, to seek advice. Beard gave it to him straight. The coaching staff, he said, had to go. Draughon agreed and fired Brown and his staff. Wilbur Hutsell was the athletic director, but he wanted to concentrate on coaching; his love was track. Draughon asked Beard to replace Hutsell and to appoint a committee to find a new football coach.

Beard already knew who he wanted. He wanted Ralph "Shug" Jordan, an assistant coach on Wally Butts's Georgia staff, who had been a tough-as-nails Auburn center. The problem was that Jordan was still seething about being passed over for the position of Auburn's head coach three years earlier when Brown had been hired. "If they don't think an Auburn man can do the job, they ought to close the joint down," Jordan said disdainfully when he learned he had not been chosen.

Beard appointed his committee, filling it with former Auburn players who knew Jordan. He asked Jordan to apply, but Jordan resisted. He didn't want to be embarrassed again. Finally, Jordan wrote a one-sentence letter: "I hereby apply for the coaching job at Auburn. Sincerely, Ralph Jordan." It was enough. Jordan was chosen over Bowden Wyatt and Norman "Shorty" Cooper. His salary would be $12,000 a year. Shortly after midnight on February 26, 1951, Beard and Jordan walked onto the front porch of the president's mansion. Hundreds of students were in the yard. Beard told them Jordan would be Auburn's next football coach. The students cheered, and Auburn would never be the same.

The Shug Jordan Story

Ralph Jordan, the son of a railroad man, was born September 25, 1910, in Selma. His childhood love for sugar cane earned him the nickname "Shug." He tasted his first athletic success at the Selma YMCA, where coach Paul Grist had a major impact on his life. Jordan arrived in Auburn in 1928. It quickly became established that he was an outstanding athlete, lettering in football as a center, in basketball as a guard, and in baseball as a pitcher. Shortly after he graduated, Jordan went to work for his old Auburn football coach, Chet Wynne, as an assistant freshman coach. When Jack Meagher replaced Wynne, Jordan stayed on. In a day when assistant football coaches often coached other sports, Jordan was Auburn's head basketball coach before he was its head football coach.

Jordan's career was interrupted when his country called him to duty. As a decorated army lieutenant, he was wounded in the invasion of Normandy on D-Day. He also participated in major invasions in North Africa, Sicily, and Okinawa. Jordan came home in 1945 and coached one more year at Auburn before leaving to join Meagher's staff with the professional Miami Seahawks. With the Seahawks falling apart, Jordan went to work for Wally Butts at Georgia, setting in motion the events that led him back to the alma mater he loved.

When Jordan arrived at Auburn, he took over a program that could scarcely have been in worse shape. Vince Dooley, who would become a great quarterback for Jordan and later have a legendary career of his own at Georgia, was an Auburn freshman in 1950. According to Dooley, "What I saw in my freshman year was probably the worst football team I've ever seen, and a poorly coached

Ralph "Shug" Jordan, Auburn's beloved coach, known for both his integrity and record number of wins.

team, I might add. I absolutely felt like my high school could have played them a heck of a game. Losing to Wofford was one thing, then we lost to Southeast Louisiana. I thought that was the worst game I'd ever seen and still feel that way. I was pretty discouraged, as you might imagine, with that. That's when Coach Jordan came."

Over the next twenty-five years, Jordan won 176 games, lost 83, and tied 6. He won the 1957 national championship. He made Auburn's name great again in the world of college football. He was inducted into the National Football Foundation Hall of Fame and the Alabama Sports Hall of Fame. In 1973 Cliff Hare Stadium officially became Jordan-Hare Stadium. Today, Shug Jordan Parkway runs by the Auburn campus.

The Tigers shocked heavily favored Vanderbilt 24–14 in Jordan's first game and finished 5–5 in 1951. After falling back to 2–8 in 1952, the Tigers began a surge that would culminate with a 10–0 record and the 1957 national championship. Starting with a 27–20 win over Mississippi State in 1956, they went twenty-four games without a loss.

Along the way, Jordan became known as one of the true gentlemen of college football. The men who played for him still talk of the lessons he taught. "He earned your respect because of the way he handled himself and conducted himself," recalled Mike Kolen, an All-Southeastern Conference linebacker who went on to great days with the Miami Dolphins. "He was just a class guy. Being the kind of person he was, he earned the respect of his players. We were fortunate to have the opportunity to play for him." Jordan, true to his Selma roots, was gracious in victory and defeat. He was humble and had no need for the spotlight. His telephone number was listed for all to see.

Ralph Jordan Jr., who lives near Knoxville, Tennessee, and is senior resource specialist with the Tennessee Valley Authority, remembers a simple man in simpler and gentler times. He says his father would not have been comfortable under the searing spotlight that shines on today's coaches in big-time college football, nor would he have been able to comprehend football coaches making $2 million a year. "There's been such a transition in coaching," Ralph Jr. says. "He went to see his barber every week to get his hair cut. That was almost a ritual. He didn't have any problems with fans. He would stop and talk to people and people would talk to him. That's the way he wanted it. Occasionally, we would have a fan call up in the middle of the night in unforgiving terms, but it was an unusual occurrence. Everybody knew the number. All you had to do was pick up the phone and tell the operator who you wanted. People were a lot more forgiving then. I think the fans have changed, and it's not a good change."

Jordan's graciousness belied the competitive fires that burned hot in his gut. His voice could be like a warm embrace or icy with anger. Steve Wilson, now a prominent Huntsville lawyer, was Jordan's kind of player. He walked on, beat the odds, and became the undersized linebacker who earned the respect of teammates and opponents. He remembers one day in 1970 when Jordan got his players' attention. The Tigers had beaten Tennessee 36–23 in a monumental showdown a week earlier. Expected to win easily at Kentucky, they trailed 9–0 at halftime. "We got in the locker room and the offense was on one side and the defense on the other," Wilson remembers. "There was nobody else in the room. We knew the coaches were out there because we could hear them talking, but nobody came in to talk to us. All of a sudden, there is a loud bang. Coach Jordan literally kicks the door off the hinges. He takes three steps with his arms crossed, and the managers and coaches walk in behind him. He starts tugging on that ear, and you know all hell is about to break loose. He looks all around the room and doesn't say a word. Then he looks up and he has a really disgusted look on his face. He says 'You stink worse than stale s—.' He didn't say another word. He walked out of the locker room and everybody went with him. Wallace Clark ran the kickoff back for a touchdown and we won 33–15."

As times changed and players changed, Jordan tried to adapt. But his core values—faith, family, hard work, and loyalty—never wavered. Jordan's reach extended far beyond the football field. David Housel grew up an Auburn fan in Gordo, just down the road from the University of Alabama. When he enrolled as a journalism student at Auburn and worked in the publicity office, he came to know Jordan. Housel went on to be assistant ticket manager, sports information director, and finally athletic director. Jordan showed him the way: "Coach Jordan is the man of my life. He taught me more in four years than I got in twenty years of formal education. There may have been better coaches. There may have been coaches who won more games. But no coach meant more to his alma mater or understood his values more than Coach Jordan. He laid the foundation for his school—the intangibles, his values. His sense of purpose meant more than anything."

There was no room for compromise in Jordan's values, on the football field, in the community, in his home. "If he ever told me a lie, I don't remember it," says Ralph Jr. "There were times I didn't want to listen and times I didn't believe what he told me. I know today what he told me was true and I damned well should have listened to him. That, to me, is what coaching is all about. Anybody can get out there and threaten to take people's scholarships away."

When Terry Henley had trouble with fumbles early in his career, Jordan didn't give up on him. Jordan didn't like Henley's outspoken ways, but he loved him. As a senior in 1972, Henley was the hard-nosed tailback who refused to fumble as Auburn went 10–1. "He was my buddy, my friend, the daddy I never had," Henley says. "I could go to his house and talk to him. I could go to the office and talk to him. He knew I had a mother at home raising my two brothers. He was very special to me, and I hope I was very special to him. He didn't like my long hair and he didn't like some of the comments I made, but he accepted me anyway."

Joe Connally was at Jordan's side every step of the way at Auburn. When Jordan was named Auburn's head coach in 1951, he hired Connally, who was a high school coach in Decatur, Georgia. Connally never left and is now retired and living in Auburn. Jordan's greatest strength, according to Connally, was his ability to understand people and to feel what they felt. "He was just kind of a fair person without having to work at it," Connally says. "He was tough enough when he had to be tough and he was easy when he needed to be easy. He knew how to handle situations and handle people. He didn't let any situation get away from him."

Jordan never won another championship after 1957, but he must have set a record for near misses. The Tigers finished second in the Southeastern Conference (SEC) in 1955, 1958, 1963, 1965, 1971, 1972, and 1974. In three other seasons, they were a win away from finishing on top. The 1972 team didn't win a championship only because Alabama played one more SEC game.

Shug Jordan on
the sideline.

In spring 1975 Jordan shocked the state when he announced that season would be his last. The Tigers had gone 10–2 in 1974, and big things were expected in 1975. The Tigers staggered to a 3–6–2 record. Jordan, hurting inside, handled it as he always handled adversity, with grace and dignity. On November 29, 1975, Jordan coached his last Auburn game, a 28–0 loss to Alabama in Birmingham. Housel was an Auburn journalism instructor at the time, but he was like part of the Jordan family. "It really wasn't as emotional as most people think," Housel recalls. "Most of the emotion was gone by then. When you are in the eye of the storm, it's not as strong as when you are outside it. He'd come to grips with that being his last season long before that week. I think he was looking forward to retiring and living the rest of his life." According to Ralph Jr., in the end, his father could look back on it all and see a job well done. "I never detected any note of regret," Ralph Jr. says. "I think he felt they did everything they could and that they won with class and integrity."

In 1976 Jordan was appointed to the Auburn Board of Trustees, an astonishing honor for a football coach. He served until he died on July 17, 1980. Stricken with leukemia, Jordan died as he lived—quietly, gracefully, and courageously. "He died in his sleep, which was a blessing," Ralph Jr. said. "It was a real dark time for us. He was the one you always turned to in a crisis. He'd always been there. It took us all a while to get our feet under us. Just as we were settling into a relationship of one man to another, he was gone. I feel like I was robbed." No Auburn coach before or since has approached Jordan's record of 176 wins. It isn't likely anyone will. Jordan and his wife, Evelyn, never sought the perks and bright lights they could have had. They were content to raise their children, Ralph Jr., Susan, and Darby, and enjoy life in the college town they loved.

"You know, he kept every sideline pass, Ralph Jr. says. "We had two ceramic tigers that sat on the bookshelf in the living room. We had a winning tiger and a losing tiger. If we lost, he'd put that pass over the neck of the losing tiger. If we won, he'd tell me 'Go put this one on the winning tiger.' By the time he coached his last game, there were a lot of sideline passes on that winning tiger." But it wasn't the wins, Ralph Jr. explains, that meant the most. "I think most important is what his players have gone on to become. They are lawyers, doctors, successful people. It's hard to look at those people and not think he played a role in that. That's what he would be most proud of. They are an interesting group of people. They have remarkably high levels of integrity and honesty. There's a certain air about them. I think that's the thing he would be most proud of."

The Jeff Beard Story

Garland Washington Beard, better known as Jeff, was a standout athlete in his own right. A native of Hardinsburg, Kentucky, he was Southern Conference discus champion as a member of the Auburn track team. He graduated in 1932 and left only briefly before returning as athletics business manager and assistant track coach. From the time he became athletic director until his retirement in 1972, Beard's mission was Auburn athletics. The glittering facilities that Auburn's athletes use today might not be there had it not been for Beard's commitment in the early days. During his tenure, Beard oversaw the addition of 40,000 seats to what was

Athletic director
Jeff Beard at the
Gator Bowl.
*Ralph Draughon
Library*

then Cliff Hare Stadium. Under his guidance, the Auburn "Family" came to expect excellence where it had once learned to live with despair and even hopelessness.

When Beard was hired in February 1951, Auburn's athletics department was in dire straits. It was some $100,000 in debt, an astronomical amount for the time. Under his leadership the department was transformed from a financial drain into an enterprise that actually gave money back to the university. In the early days, when tickets were a hard sell and Auburn people were divided about supporting football, Beard and Jordan would drive to alumni meetings. Jordan would speak and Beard would sell tickets out of the trunk of his car.

Buddy Davidson arrived at Auburn as a freshman football manager in 1957. He's still there today as an assistant athletic director. Beard, he says, made a major impact on his life as a professional and as a person. "First and foremost, in his approach to running the athletic department, he did it from the standpoint of a family atmosphere. I give him a lot of credit for what we now call the Auburn Family. At that time, it was so much different from today. He was able to run it the way he thought it ought to be run. President Draughon gave him all the authority to go with the responsibility. He really kind of ran it out of his hip pocket, but he was a man of unquestioned integrity."

Kenny Howard came to Auburn as a student, became a renowned trainer, and later a senior administrator. He remembers Beard had unique qualities: "It was his ability to keep people happy. As a personnel manager, he didn't have anybody staying mad at him. He was extremely good with numbers and was an excellent business manager. He knew how to take care of the dol-

The Beard Legacy

Not long after Jeff Beard became athletic director in 1951, he went to see a university committee with a proposal to upgrade some of Auburn's athletics facilities. They quickly asked how much it would cost. Beard told them it would cost less than $1,000 and that it would be paid for out of the next year's gate receipts. The committee laughed at him, pointing out that the athletic department had never made any money. They didn't believe it ever would. Beard pressed on anyway. When he retired after twenty-two years, he had raised Auburn's athletic department from the ashes of despair.

David Housel, who would later become athletic director himself, wrote:

> Since the day Coach Beard announced his retirement, his accomplishments and contributions have been chronicled again and again. Here, for the record, they are once more: More than 40,000 additional seats in Cliff Hare Stadium, Memorial Coliseum, Sewell Hall, Hutsell Track, a financially sound athletic program and, most important, a composite team record of 1,442 victories against 670 defeats in all sports. This is the tangible evidence of Jeff Beard's twenty-one-year labor of love and devotion, but perhaps his greatest accomplishment was one of morale. He brought Auburn back from the worst kind of despair, a depression of spirit, a hopelessness that permeated every aspect of Auburn's athletic program.

lars and how to make the dollars grow." Like Jordan, Beard's gracious ways belied the toughness inside. "He was a pretty tough, demanding man that insisted on good, quality coaches," Howard says. "He was able to select quality people and keep them happy. He held a tight rein on the budget. People said he was tight with the money, and he was. That was one of his greatest assets."

Beard and Jordan were more than partners in a great adventure. They were warm and close friends. They first met as members of opposing high school basketball teams. Beard played at Greensboro and Jordan at Selma. They started out together as freshmen on the 1928 Auburn football team. Beard had never seen a football game until his senior year in high school, but he wanted to play at Auburn. It didn't work. "I almost got killed," Beard admitted years later. Instead, he concentrated on track.

Beard died in 1995. His leadership was felt through the SEC and college football. His name is on Auburn's basketball arena, Beard-Eaves Memorial Coliseum, and he is a member of the Alabama Sports Hall of Fame.

National Champions

There was no talk of a national championship as Auburn's football team went off to Knoxville, Tennessee, to start the 1957 season. Sure, most expected the Tigers to be good. They'd gotten progressively stronger since Shug Jordan took over as head coach in 1951, going 29–9–1 over the previous four seasons. They'd even finished number eight at the end of the 1955 season. But a national championship? Most observers didn't even give the Tigers a chance to beat Tennessee.

A year earlier, the Tigers and the Vols had resumed a long-dormant series at Birmingham's Legion Field. Tennessee coach Robert Neyland had been opposed to playing Auburn, believing his team had nothing to gain. In the first game of 1956, it seemed he had been right. The Vols had won 35–7 at Birmingham's Legion Field in the first meeting between the two teams since 1939.

On September 28, 1957, Auburn shocked Tennessee 7–0 on a cold, rainy day at Shields-Watkins Field. The most memorable run in Auburn football history had begun. Jimmy "Red" Phillips, the team captain who came from Alexander City and became one of Auburn's all-time greats and an NFL star, says the Tigers were confident as preseason practice began. But there was nothing to indicate what was to come. "We had no idea," Phillips recalls. "We expected to win. We were used to winning, but nobody was talking about national championships or even an SEC championship. We were just trying to do what our coaches wanted."

Phillips, listed at 210 pounds but actually closer to 190, was one of the bigger players on the team. The days of 300-pound linemen and 250-pound linebackers were still years away. Auburn players were small even by the standards of the time. But Auburn had a defense that still stands as one of the great units in the history of the game. The Tigers gave up just 28 points—four touchdowns—all season. One was on an interception return, and three came against the second-team defense. Mississippi State was the only SEC team that managed to score, losing 15–7. The Tigers went 10–0 and, over the vehement protests of Ohio State coach Woody Hayes, were the landslide choice as national champion in the Associated Press poll.

As practice began on September 1, there were so many questions and so few answers. At the end of spring practice, Jimmy Cook had been the starting quarterback and Donnie May the starting fullback. Both had left school and would not be part of the 1957 football team. Three weeks before the opener, Jordan announced that Lloyd Nix would be the starting quarterback. Nix, a junior left-hander, had been a second-string halfback. He wore 44 and had not played quarterback since his days at Carbon Hill High School. He was not particularly fast or particularly strong.

"I'm not worried about Lloyd's ability to get the job done," Jordan said in making the announcement that Nix would start. "He has game experience, and he has the mental qualities and natural poise to be a good quarterback. He's not flashy, but he gets the job done and that's what counts." Nix was, more than anything else, a winner who seldom made mistakes. He would finish his career without losing a game as a starting quarterback. Untested Billy "Ace" Atkins stepped into the void left by May at fullback. He had a nose for the end zone, scoring 11 touchdowns, which was then a school record. Halfback Tommy Lorino was already a star and had led the Southeastern Conference in rushing in 1956. Bobby Hoppe, the other halfback, was a speedster.

"I went home for the summer and planned on going back as a halfback," says Nix, now a retired dentist in Decatur, Alabama. "When Coach Jordan told me I was moving to quarterback, it wasn't that big a deal. I was getting to play, and that was all that mattered. They talk about how we couldn't throw, we couldn't do

Red Phillips (88), Bobby Hoppe (20), and Tommy Lorino (25) with Jordan.

this, couldn't do that. If our offensive mindset had been such, we could really have put some points on the board. We just kind of threw it when we had to. As soon as we scored, we knew we were going to win."

It was defense that was the 1957 team's trademark. Phillips, right end Jerry Wilson, Lorino, and Nix were established defensive players in that day of two-way football. Little did anyone know that two of the great linemen in Auburn history were also in camp. Linebacker/center Jackie Burkett and guard Zeke Smith were both red-shirt sophomores. Both became All-Americans, and Smith won the Outland Trophy in 1958.

Burkett was star quarterback at Shalimar High School in Fort Walton Beach, Florida. As he neared the end of his senior year in 1955, he planned to play for Alabama. "I'd already told Alabama I was going over there, but I had not visited Auburn," Burkett recollects. His high school coach, Hal Wyatt, was an Auburn graduate. He asked Burkett to give Auburn a look before signing. Burkett reluctantly agreed. "Nothing he said caused me to go to Auburn, but he did cause me to visit," Burkett says. "Once I visited, I knew that's where I wanted to go. It worked out. If I'd gone to Alabama, I'd have probably been a quarterback and I don't know if I would have played much." He also would not have won a national championship. "The experiences I had at Auburn have done wonderful things for me," Burkett reflects. "They have taught me in my business life, helped me in making contacts with people. My association with former teammates has been wonderful. I wouldn't change a thing."

Burkett's quarterback days ended before his freshman season. He and Smith were both centers. After a red-shirt year in 1956, Smith was moved to guard and they formed the South's top offensive line duo. "I got up there and accepted it," Burkett says. "I was more interested in doing what the coaches wanted me to do. They seemed to think I was better at playing center and linebacker. I'd say they were right." Burkett moved to center because the center played linebacker on offense. "Zeke was a center, too, our freshman year," Burkett remembers. "They moved him to guard after our red-shirt year, and I'd say it worked out pretty well."

Smith went to Auburn from little Uniontown, Alabama, in 1955 as a fullback. He wasn't highly recruited. He managed to get to Auburn because his father, Morgan Smith, worked for Southern Railroad with Jordan's father. "I wasn't recruited much," recalls Smith, who played five years of professional football and retired after a highly successful sales career in Birmingham. "People said they weren't taking players from little schools. I just wanted to go somewhere they would give me a scholarship. Coach Jordan's daddy and my daddy talked about it. Coach Jordan's daddy talked to Coach Jordan. That's how I ended up at Auburn."

Smith's given name was Roger, but he became Zeke when his high school coach said he ran like Georgia quarterback Zeke Bratkowski. Smith had been a star at Uniontown, but once he got to Auburn, he was awed by what he saw. "I'd never seen so many good players in one place," Smith says. "At Uniontown, some of the guys that were playing would have been managers or cheerleaders." At Auburn, Zeke became one of the great linemen in Southern football history, but he almost didn't even get to his first game. Smith admits, "I got discouraged several times and started to quit. I'd get up the next day and say 'If this guy can stay, I can, too.' I just kept hanging in there. Practice was really rough."

Hal Herring, a former Auburn and NFL star, was the mad scientist behind the Auburn defense. He designed different defenses for different teams. "My philosophy was to tackle the guy with the ball, cover the guy they throw to, and don't cover those decoys," Herring says. Auburn's defense had no fancy name. It wasn't needed. "Nobody could figure out what it was, including me," Herring concedes. "I adopted some stuff we used in pro ball. Some things I tinkered with. I tailored each defense for each game."

Buddy Davidson was a freshman manager in 1957, and he saw that defense up close day in and day out. "Managers refereed the scrimmages," recalls Davidson, now an assistant athletic director at Auburn. "They scrimmaged almost every day. They'd put the ball on the 3 yard line and put the first defense against the second offense. They'd give them four downs to score. They haven't scored yet, and that's the whole season. Ball control, running the clock, the kicking game, all those things were more focal points of the game. You didn't see anybody throwing on first down from their own 2. It just didn't happen. It was just me against you, man on man." The specialized coaching, conditioning, and weight training that are so much a part of the modern game played no role in 1957. Auburn had no weight room. It didn't even have any weights. Practices were long and grueling, half spent on offense and half on defense. Joel Eaves, the head basketball coach, coached defensive ends. Gene Lorendo coached offensive ends, Buck Bradberry the backfield, and Shot Senn the line. Vince Dooley was assistant backfield coach and George Atkins assistant line coach. Dick McGowen and Joe Connally were freshman coaches.

The real story of the 1957 team was about heart, determination, and devotion to duty and to each other. As Herring acknowledges, "I give all the credit to the players because they listened to what was going on. We didn't have a quarterback, and Joel Eaves suggested that Lloyd Nix had played there in high school. It was unheard of for a defensive guy to suggest something to the offense. It turned out Lloyd was a very innovative quarterback.

You had Lorino, Atkins, and Hoppe in the backfield. All of them could run. It just worked out. You had guys who paid attention to what you were doing. You could plan things, and they were going to do what you wanted them to do."

At Tennessee, Auburn drove 62 yards on its first possession, but the threat died at the Tennessee 1. Later in the first quarter, Atkins missed a short field goal. In the second quarter, the Tigers drove 57 yards. This time, Atkins got it in from the 1 and kicked the extra point. Auburn had all the points it needed. "That game was a real key," Nix admits. "Lorino had an awful day against them in 1956. He fumbled on the kickoff and just had a bad day. We go up there and beat Tennessee in the rain, don't make mistakes. They probably sort of see I'm not going to give the game away at quarterback. You've got Burkett, Phillips, Wilson, Zeke, and all those guys. It just sort of grows as we go along."

It was a sign of things to come. The Tigers didn't score a lot, but they didn't need to score a lot. According to Smith, "We knew once we had a touchdown or even a field goal that we were going to win. We didn't believe anybody could score on us, and most people couldn't." Unranked in the preseason, Auburn jumped to number seven in the next week's Associated Press poll. The climb to a championship had begun.

The Tigers routed Chattanooga 40–7, then took on Kentucky and tackle Lou Michaels. "It was as tough and hard-hitting as any game I ever played in," Smith says. "I had to try to block Michaels all day. And I stress the word *try*." The game seemed headed for a scoreless tie when Michaels was called for a personal foul for throwing a forearm at Lorino. Auburn took advantage and Atkins got the ball into the end zone. Auburn won 6–0.

They Were Champions, Too

Though only the 1957 team is widely regarded as a national champion, five other Auburn teams were also named national champions. Here are the other teams and who ranked them at the top of college football's mountain:

> 1910 (6–1): Billingsley Report
> 1913 (8–0): Billingsley Report
> 1983 (11–1): The *New York Times*, College Football Research Association, FACT, and Massey.
> 1993 (11–0): National Championship Foundation.
> 2004 (13–0): People's National Championship poll, numerous computer polls.

Atkins kicked a field goal for the game's only points, and Auburn beat ancient rival Georgia Tech to move to number five in the poll.

Auburn ran its record to 5–0 with a 48–7 blitz of Houston, scoring on the game's first play on a 70-yard pass from Nix to Phillips. The Tigers dominated Florida 13–0 and were heavily favored against Mississippi State in Birmingham. But the Maroons put Auburn behind for the first time, leading 7–0 at halftime. After a paint-peeling speech by Jordan at halftime, the Tigers went out and took control. They dominated the second half, winning 15–7, and climbed to number three in the AP poll. Oklahoma was number one and Texas A&M was number two.

As the Tigers prepared for their annual showdown against Georgia in Columbus, Jordan talked to his players about the national championship for the first time. They beat Georgia 6–0 on a touchdown pass from Nix to Phillips. Nix remembers a frightening moment that day. He was running an option and pitched toward Lorino. "We were down inside our 20 and the grass was a little wet," Nix recalls excitedly. "I threw the ball behind Lorino and he slips coming back to get it. Georgia recovers." As the players prepared to play defense, Smith patted Nix on the back and gave him a big smile. "Don't worry, Lloyd, I'll get it back," Smith told his quarterback. "Sure enough, he made the guy fumble on the next play and recovered the fumble," Nix says.

While the Tigers and Bulldogs played, Notre Dame knocked off number one Oklahoma 7–0, ending the Sooners' forty-seven-game winning streak. Rice upset Texas A&M 7–6. The path was clear for Auburn, or so it seemed. It was then that players first began to hear talk of a national championship. "We were working too hard to think about it," Nix recalls. "Coach Jordan was a great guy, but his assistants just worked the stew out of you. We heard that Oklahoma had lost, and that was good for us. I remember Coach Jordan saying before the Alabama game, 'Guys, y'all have a good game against Alabama, you have a chance to win the national championship.'" But when the poll came out, Michigan State had jumped from number four to number one. Auburn was number two.

On November 23, Auburn whipped Florida State 29–7. Michigan State beat Kansas State but was unimpressive in doing it. On Monday, Auburn ascended to number one in the poll. Once-beaten Ohio State was number two, and Buckeye coach

Woody Hayes was campaigning hard for his team. Auburn made a powerful point against Alabama. Lorino and Burkett returned interceptions for touchdowns. The Tigers routed the Tide 40–0 in the final game of J. B. "Ears" Whitworth's tenure as head coach.

Late on the afternoon of Monday, December 2, Auburn publicist Bill Beckwith got the happy word. Auburn was number one in all the land. Sound trucks broadcast the news across campus. Auburn had 8,000 students, and most of them showed up at Ross Square for a celebration. Jordan climbed the steps of the Ross Chemistry Building to talk to the roaring students.

"As far as I'm concerned, Auburn has been No. 1 all year," Jordan bellowed over the crowd. "I want to thank all the people

Auburn receives the 1957 National Championship trophy.

all over the nation who went to bat for the Tigers in the poll. Let me tell you something else: This is an honor for this school and this student body. The Auburn football team is no different from those of you here today. Being No. 1 is something for us all."

Burkett says it would be years later before he realized the full impact of what he and his teammates had done. "We were trying to win some games and I was trying to have a good time," says Burkett, who was 6'4" and at the time weighed 215 pounds. "We didn't really realize how significant it was at the time. We knew winning the national championship was special, but we didn't know how special."

There was no bowl game, however. Auburn was serving the first of four years of NCAA probation. In those days, it was little more than an irritant. "I don't remember anybody talking about it much," says Nix. "We all knew what the situation was when we went there. It wasn't a very big deal." A year before Jordan arrived, Auburn had been 0–10. In his seventh season, Auburn was 10–0. Auburn football had reached its all-time high.

The men who won a championship almost a half century ago are still proud today of what they did. They'll tell you still that those were the best days of their lives. "Go back and look at the character of those guys and how they have lived their lives," Nix says. "They've been successful, good citizens. A big thing is they wanted to play for Auburn. Everybody knew they had a job to do. It wasn't a rah-rah kind of deal. One way or another, it was going to get done."

Nobody worried about individual statistics. Lorino, who had led the SEC in rushing in 1956, didn't even have ten carries a game. "There were so many close games," says Lorino, who officiated in the SEC for twenty-four years and now owns Golden Rule Barbecue in Auburn. "It was nip and tuck. We'd run Ace twice and me once and punt. Bobby Hoppe and I were supposed to be the premier running backs in the South. Against Georgia Tech, I think I ran it four times and he ran it three."

What mattered was winning. And the Tigers of 1957 won them all. "Those days at Auburn were some of the greatest days of my life," Smith says in retrospect. "The national championship was great. That was about as big as it gets. That's something to strut about."

Pat and Bo

By twenty-first-century standards, Pat Sullivan's statistics aren't overwhelming, but they were stunning in 1971. He tied an NCAA record for touchdown responsibility with 71. His 53 career touchdown passes were the third best in NCAA history. His total offense average of 228.1 yards per game set an NCAA record. But more than numbers on a page, Sullivan's legacy was one of leadership and grace under fire. He welcomed the opportunity carried by the few who are called on to show the way. "I've never seen Pat worried, not even when we're behind," fullback Wallace Clark said as Sullivan headed into his senior season. "Concerned? Yes. Worried? No. He knows how to win, how to come back when he gets behind. And he always keeps the pressure on the other team when we get the upper hand. Being behind only makes Pat watch himself more."

As the 1971 season headed toward the home stretch, Auburn, Alabama, Georgia, Oklahoma, and Nebraska established themselves as contenders for the national championship. Sullivan, who as a junior had finished sixth in the 1970 Heisman balloting, was the leading contender for the trophy. Ralph Jordan, Sullivan's coach and friend, called Sullivan "the most complete quarterback I've ever seen. When he's in the game, there's not one thing your offense is not capable of doing." Paul Bryant, who tried hard to recruit Sullivan out of Birmingham's John Carroll High School, added his praise: "He does more to beat you than any quarterback I've ever seen."

As the season wore on and Auburn won game after game, Sullivan felt mounting pressure to lead his team to victories and to deal with the Heisman hype. Sports information director Buddy Davidson became a friend and confidant. Now back home in Birmingham as offensive coordinator at UAB, Sullivan recalls how Davidson helped him through the hardest times. "There were a lot of distractions," Sullivan admits. "Buddy did a great job of keeping everything organized. People talked as much about the Heisman as they did about our season. Every day there was some kind of media thing. It really wore on me."

Pat Sullivan takes
a break.

Sullivan fought on and, when it was over, he stood where no Auburn football player had ever stood. On November 25, 1971, he was named the Heisman Trophy winner. Fourteen years later, in 1985, running back Bo Jackson became the second Auburn player to claim this coveted award in college athletics. Back in 1971, however, the announcement of the Heisman Trophy winner was not the media extravaganza it is today. Contenders weren't invited to New York for the opening of the envelope. Jackson was at the Downtown Athletic Club when it was announced he had won. Sullivan watched on television with his wife, his parents, and close friends at the Heart of Auburn Motel.

To this day, Sullivan's teammates say he was the ultimate team player and leader. When he missed a day of Gator Bowl practice in 1970 to accept the Southeastern Conference Player of the Year Award in Nashville, he apologized when he returned. "You all read the papers and you know where I was," Sullivan told them. "I'm sorry I had to go during practice, but I want you to know I didn't accept the award for me. I accepted it for you. Any praise or credit I got doesn't belong to me. It belongs to you, and I thank you for letting me be your representative." As November arrived Sullivan and record-setting Cornell running back Ed Marinaro were the leading candidates for the Heisman. There was significant sentiment for Marinaro, because the Ivy League had been so long out of the spotlight.

Just as Jackson would do in 1985, Sullivan stepped to the front against Georgia at Sanford Stadium in Athens. Auburn went into the game 8–0 and ranked number six. Georgia was 9–0 and ranked number seven. By any measure, it was as big a game as Auburn had ever played—the latest in the season that two unbeaten SEC teams had ever met. The atmosphere was electric. "The hype of the game and the atmosphere were unbelievable," Sullivan remembers. "We rode the bus over, and 20 or 30 miles outside of town the Georgia students met us and started circling the buses. They were shouting things, throwing beer cans, all kinds of stuff. Once all that started, you could have heard a pin drop on the bus."

Georgia students kept it up at the Auburn team hotel, circling the building in cars and honking horns until early in the morning. Auburn offensive coordinator Gene Lorendo, a giant of a man who had played on the offensive line at Auburn, caught one student banging on a player's door. The student escaped by scooting between Lorendo's legs and sprinting away. Sullivan had an answer the next day, November 13. He completed 14 of 24 passes for 248 yards and 4 touchdowns. Auburn won 35–20 to set up an even bigger game against unbeaten Alabama.

But first there was the Heisman Trophy. The announcement came on Thanksgiving night at halftime of the Georgia-Georgia Tech game. When the big moment finally arrived, Sullivan was named the winner. Sullivan accepted the news as he had everything else, with calm, class, and grace. His teammates and Auburn students celebrated wildly. Two days later, Auburn's dream of a national championship died in a 31–7 loss to Alabama, to this day a bitter memory for Auburn players who were there. Sullivan believes his team lost its emotional edge with the Heisman announcement. On January 1, 1972, in Sullivan's final game, Auburn lost 40–22 to Oklahoma in the Sugar

Bowl. "Oklahoma was better than we were, pure and simple," Sullivan admits. "Alabama wasn't. I'm not saying we would have beaten Alabama, but our senior class had never lost to them. We didn't play very well."

. . .

On December 13, 1985, Sullivan sat with other former winners as Bo Jackson stood to formally accept the trophy at New York's hallowed Downtown Athletic Club. As Jackson stepped back from the podium, his speech completed, there was routine applause. The applause grew louder until, finally, those in the audience were standing and cheering. The poor kid from Bessemer who once had seemed almost certainly headed for reform school was now standing at the top of the college football world, proclaimed the best in the land.

Jackson, the eighth of Florence Bond's ten children, had grown up in a little house in Bessemer. Now, here he was decked out in a tuxedo and living the dream of countless boys. "My mom raised us in a three-room house," Jackson told those gathered to honor him. "The house consisted of a kitchen, where my mom had her bedroom; a living room, which had a gas heater; and a bedroom that had a potbellied stove and twin beds. As children, we slept wherever we could find a vacant place in the house. And the majority of the time I would get down right in front of the little gas heater in the living room. Some nights I didn't have a cover to put over me, but I knew my mom would take care of me." Jackson says that nothing he accomplished playing football could compare with the warmth he felt when his mother came in the night and covered him with a blanket. "I don't care about

Zeke, Tracy, and Carlos

Though Bo Jackson and Pat Sullivan stand alone as the only Auburn players ever to win the Heisman Trophy, others have also been honored on national stages. Two-way guard Zeke Smith won the Outland Trophy as the nation's top lineman in 1958. In 1988 defensive tackle Tracy Rocker became the only SEC player to win both the Outland Trophy and the Lombardi Award in the same season. The Lombardi Award goes to the nation's top defensive player. In 2004 Carlos Rogers won the Jim Thorpe Award as the nation's top defensive back.

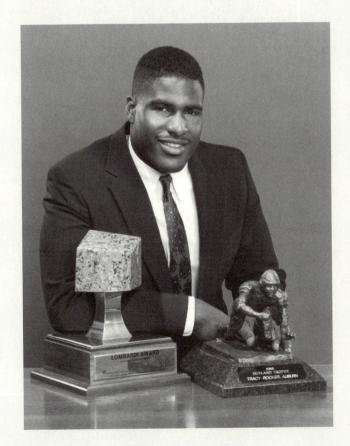

Tracy Rocker with his trophies.

all the criticism people throw at me, because I know I had harder times. Nothing can make me feel better than what I experienced growing up."

Sullivan and Jackson were different people in different times, but each lifted Auburn football in his own way. Jackson was the catalyst who helped coach Pat Dye embark on the most successful decade in Auburn football history. Sullivan and red-haired receiver Terry Beasley led a transformation into the modern ways of offensive football. David Housel, who retired as athletic director in 2004, spent thirty-five years at Auburn in various capacities. He was there to see Sullivan and Jackson reach the mountaintop. As Housel recalls, "Coach Dye said of Bo Jackson that he gave Auburn people the greatest thing in the world. He gave them hope—hope of beating Alabama, hope of building a championship football program . . . I think the same could be said of Pat Sullivan. And in Auburn history, it is impossible to talk about Pat Sullivan without talking about Terry Beasley. Together, they gave Auburn hope that Auburn had never had at that time in our history."

Jackson, 222 powerful pounds with the speed of a world-class sprinter, won the Heisman Trophy by rushing for 1,786 yards as a senior. He went on to be a star for the Kansas City Royals and Chicago White Sox and in the NFL for the Oakland Raiders. Before a hip injury cut his career short, he was a Nike marketing icon. As a student at McAdory High School near Bessemer, Jackson was "Mr. Everything" in sports, once scoring 29 points in a football game and batting just under .500 in baseball. *Birmingham News* reporter Ronald Weathers, who covered high school athletics for more than three decades, recalls that Jackson was so dominant in the state decathlon that he sat out the final event, the mile run, because he'd won the first nine. Auburn track coach Mel Rosen said later that Jackson could have been an Olympic sprinter had he chosen to concentrate on track. In 1982, as a shy freshman, Jackson turned down a $250,000 bonus from the New York Yankees, choosing instead to play football for Auburn.

Jackson was not the most heavily recruited running back in Alabama. That distinction went to Enterprise's Alan Evans, who signed with Auburn but never made a significant impact. Bobby Wallace, the assistant who recruited Jackson, knew his potential before he arrived on campus. So did Dye. After the first preseason scrimmage, everyone knew. "I'll never forget that scrimmage in the stadium," recalls Wallace, now the head coach at Temple. "There was electricity in the air. The coaches could feel it, and you could see it in the players' eyes. Everybody knew this guy was something different, the real thing."

For Jackson, the burden was heavy. As he neared the end of his freshman year, he decided he'd had enough of the expectations, enough of school, enough of it all. Between Auburn's games against Georgia and Alabama, he went to the bus station in Opelika. He wanted to go home. One bus left and then another, but Jackson never got on. Finally, at 1:30 A.M., he called Wallace. "I was sound asleep, but I woke up quick," Wallace says. "I told Bo just to go on back to the dorm and go to sleep, that I would take care of things. We worked it out the next day. Bo got his punishment like any other player would have, and there was

Vincent "Bo" Jackson could outrun or jump over virtually all defenders.

never any problem after that." Jackson's punishment was one hundred "stadiums"—running to the top of Jordan-Hare Stadium and back one hundred times. A few days later, he rushed for 114 yards and went over the top for the winning touchdown as Auburn ended ten years of frustration with a 23–22 victory over Alabama.

Even as Jackson became a nationally acclaimed football player, piling up yards and touchdowns and leading Auburn to the 1983 SEC championship, his road was bumpy. Slowed by a bad ankle, he suffered a separated shoulder against Texas in the second game of the 1984 season and missed six games. Against Alabama, with the game on the line, he was supposed to block for Brent Fullwood out of the wishbone with victory only a few feet away. But he went the wrong way, Fullwood was stopped and Auburn lost 17–15. Even in his Heisman year, Jackson endured stinging criticism after removing himself from games against Tennessee and Florida because of injuries. Auburn lost them both.

Dye staunchly defended his star runner at every turn. "Bo has always been a man who never looked back," Dye says. "He hasn't ever had to make any apologies either. That includes when he went the wrong way on the goal line and we lost to Alabama and when he came out of a couple of games because he got hurt. He caught some flak from a lot of people who didn't know what the hell they were talking about."

Jackson went into his senior year as the clear Heisman favorite, but the criticism took its toll and Iowa quarterback Chuck Long closed in fast. Playing on a bum ankle, Jackson rushed for 121 yards and scored the game-turning touchdown on a spectacular 67-yard run against Georgia. He caught two passes for 48 yards and a touchdown, and it was just enough. He won the trophy in the closest race ever.

The Tampa Bay Bucs made Jackson the first player chosen in the NFL draft, but he shocked the sports world by opting to play baseball with the Royals. He became a major league star, hitting mammoth home runs, including one in the All-Star game. Then he went back to football and ran for the Raiders as he had run for Auburn. He became perhaps the greatest two-sport professional athlete of modern times.

Jackson had a penchant for the spectacular. At Auburn, he was as big as some linemen of his day and had jaw-dropping speed. He could hit a baseball great distances and outrun men half his size in track meets. On the football field, he had few equals. He was equally adept at outrunning defenders, running through them, or jumping over them. After his injury, Jackson had hip replacement surgery and returned to play baseball, the first professional athlete ever to return from such an injury. On top of that, he hit a home run in his first at-bat.

But Jackson never liked fame. When he retired in 1994, he left happily. He chose to live in suburban Chicago with his wife and three children. "People ask me all the time if I remember this game or that game, or if I remember when I did a particular thing," Jackson says. "Of course I remember, but all those things are in my past. My career wasn't cut short by injury. My career was cut short because I wanted it to end."

Jackson's exploits are still the stuff of legend at Auburn. In the

A Man Before His Time

There are still Auburn fans who will tell you that Tucker Frederickson is the best football player in Auburn history, better than Bo Jackson, better than Pat Sullivan, better than any of them. When Auburn fans voted in 1992 on the Team of the Century, Frederickson was the leading vote-getter. Frederickson was a man before his time. He combined size, speed, power, and finesse. In 1963 and 1964 he was the best running back, the best blocking back, and the best defensive back in the Southeastern Conference. He helped lead Auburn to the Orange Bowl in 1963 and led the nation's best defense in 1964. The New York Giants made him the first player picked in the NFL draft.

"It was an accomplishment for me to be able to get a scholarship and not have my dad pay for my college education," Frederickson says. "I could have gone a lot of places, but I'd never been out of the South and I wanted to play in the South." Frederickson was a consensus All-American as a safety in 1964 and won the Jacobs Trophy as the South's best blocker. He is a member of the Alabama Sports Hall of Fame and the College Football Hall of Fame.

school's football complex, a photograph of Jackson going over the top against Alabama occupies a place of honor. His and Sullivan's Heisman Trophies are on display for all to see.

. . .

Long before he arrived at Auburn, Sullivan had displayed the leadership skills that later served him so well. He excelled in

Pat Dye (left) and Pat Sullivan (right) with Bo and the Heisman.

football and baseball. When he was twelve, he saw his first Auburn football game, selling cold drinks at Birmingham's Legion Field as Auburn beat Georgia Tech 17–14. His exploits at John Carroll with a team short on talent and numbers drew rave reviews. After John Carroll lost a road game to powerful Huntsville High School, Huntsville coach Tom Owen marveled, "Gentlemen, you just saw the finest quarterback ever to set foot on that field."

Sullivan could have gone to virtually any school in the country. Notre Dame recruited him hard. But he followed his heart and signed with Auburn. As freshmen, Sullivan and Beasley gave a sign of things to come. The Auburn freshmen trailed Alabama's freshmen 27–0 in the first half in 1968. Sullivan and Beasley led a remarkable comeback, and the Tigers won 36–27. Two years later, Sullivan drew on that experience as he led the Tigers back from a 17–0 deficit to a 33–28 victory over the Crimson Tide at Legion Field.

The Atlanta Falcons made Sullivan the first player chosen in the second round of the NFL draft. He played four seasons with the Atlanta Falcons, then briefly with the San Francisco 49ers and Washington Redskins. After a successful career in the insurance business, Sullivan returned to Auburn in 1985 as quarterback coach for Pat Dye. He watched Jackson put his name on the list of Heisman Trophy winners. Later, he became head coach at Texas Christian before returning to his hometown to coach at UAB. His brother, Joe, and son, Patrick, followed him as Auburn quarterbacks.

In 2003 Sullivan faced the challenge of his life. He was diagnosed with cancer, squamous cell carcinoma, in the jaw and lower part of his tongue. It was the apparent result of years of using smokeless tobacco. Those closest to him saw him on the brink of death. And they saw the fighting spirit that made him an Auburn hero. Even as hope seemed to fade, he refused to give in. By the start of the 2004 season, Sullivan was back on the sideline at UAB, the cancer beaten. Today, he talks to all who will listen about the dangers of smokeless tobacco.

For those who were there when Sullivan wore number 7, he will always be the epitome of an Auburn football player. He was the star and the leader, the man to whom they all looked in the toughest times. But most of all he was a teammate. Twenty years after he won the Heisman, Sullivan was in New York to be honored again. He was one of fifteen players and coaches inducted into the National Football Foundation Hall of Fame. The other players chose Sullivan to speak for them. "It's a special honor and privilege and special responsibility for me to stand before you on behalf of the inductees," Sullivan began. "It's a responsibility I do not take lightly. None of us started out years ago with thoughts of making it to the Hall of Fame. For us to stand before you is an honor, but also a humbling experience. To know that our names and exploits will be recorded along those who have gone before us is a humbling experience. All of us are here tonight to renew our commitment to give something back to the game that has given so much to each of us."

Jackson's number 34, Sullivan's number 7, and Beasley's number 88 jerseys hang in places of honor now, retired and never to be worn again by Auburn football players. All are members of the National Football Foundation Hall of Fame. Generations of players have been inspired by their stories and have tried to climb that same mountain. None of them have made it yet.

Punt Bama Punt

Bill Newton had played the game of his life. The junior linebacker, who had come to Auburn as a walk-on, had spearheaded the Tiger defense against Alabama's powerful wishbone throughout the afternoon of December 2, 1972. But it seemed it would all go for naught. Auburn's offense had been defused since an early drive ended in a botched field-goal attempt. As the scoreboard clock at Birmingham's Legion Field raced past the ten-minute mark in the fourth quarter, Alabama, about to embark on a run of excellence that would make Bear Bryant perhaps the most revered coach in college football history, led 16–0. "You never give up," Newton says, "but it wasn't looking too good around that time."

It wasn't looking too good for Auburn football in general after the 1971 season. Pat Sullivan had won the Heisman Trophy as Auburn's quarterback in 1971. He and Terry Beasley, his favorite receiver, had gone on to the NFL. As the 1972 season neared, Auburn was written off as yesterday's news. Most pundits figured the Tigers to win three games, if that many.

Jordan knew better. Long before beat writers and saturation coverage, Jordan had put his players through off-season workouts and a spring practice so difficult and so demanding that many thought better of playing college football. Those who stayed believed they could meet any challenge. Players remember it was the second day, maybe the third. Jordan gave the offense three plays, all runs, from which to choose. The defense knew what was coming. It didn't matter. For the equivalent of two full games, players went at one another. Through the sweat and the blood, they came together. A bond grew that is still strong more than thirty years later.

"What was great about it was the closeness of that team," Newton recalls. "It started in the spring. It was tough. The coaches were trying to find out what was left. Nobody had a red shirt on. Everybody got hit." The pass-oriented attack that had taken Sullivan to the Heisman Trophy had been ditched. Auburn ran the I-formation, passing only when necessary, but when quarterback David Lyons and tailback Harry Unger were benched for injuries, it seemed there just wouldn't be enough weapons.

Gangly sophomore Randy Walls, whose forte was not making mistakes, took over at quarterback. Senior Terry Henley became the starting tailback. He ran behind bruising fullback James Owens and a hard-nosed offensive line, led by tackle Mac Lorendo. When the Tigers needed to pass, Thomas Gossom was the receiver of choice. Defensive rover Mike Neel, ends Danny Sanspree and Rusty Deen, future All-America linebacker Ken Bernich, and defensive backs Dave Beck and Johnny Simmons led a defense that found a way to make big plays at crucial times.

The Tigers would run the ball, play fierce defense, and punt. That was the plan. It was Jordan's kind of game. And it was the kind of game they prepared to play in the brutal spring of '72. No player more epitomized the 1972 Tigers than Walls. The first time he saw Sullivan throw a pass in practice, he wondered if he might not be better off back home in Brundidge. "My first thought was 'I'm in the wrong place,'" Walls remembers. "And to see Beasley running out there, I was so in awe coming from this little, bitty school down in Brundidge."

Walls was a freshman, ineligible to play under the rules of the time. It was the summer of 1971. "I knew I had a lot of improving to do," Walls says. "I realized that once I saw Pat throw the ball." Walls was a blue-collar quarterback. Statistics weren't his thing. Winning was. "As soon as I found out I was going to be the starting quarterback, I knew we weren't going to be the same football team or run the same offense. In that respect, the pressure wasn't there. We weren't going to throw the ball."

An Auburn Pioneer

The year was 1969. James Owens, one of Eloise and Neal Owens's eight children, was a freshman Auburn football player, but he wasn't just any player. He was the only African-American Auburn football player, the first one in school history. He'd left the warm embrace of his family in Fairfield for this strange new world, one that would test him as he'd never been tested before.

"For four years, every day that I got up, the first thing I'd do is look in the mirror and say 'I'm going home today. This is the day I leave here,'" Owens recalls. "I'd call my mom and tell her I was coming home. She'd encourage me and tell me not to quit, not to give up. It was hard. You are with your family, and then you are snatched away and placed in a totally different environment. We had such a strong family relationship, and all of a sudden I didn't see them. My parents were rooted and grounded in the church. They really, really prayed. With me, it took a whole lot of it."

Owens persevered and it paid off. He was one of the heroes on the 1972 team, the fast and powerful fullback who led the way for tailback Terry Henley. Many of his teammates say to this day that, given the chance, he would have been one of the top tailbacks in Auburn history. Today, Owens is the pastor at Pleasant Ridge Missionary Baptist Church in Dadeville and is assistant manager in the fielding and services division at Auburn. He says he is grateful now for his experience, proud that he helped open long-closed doors to African-American athletes. He is at peace with himself.

"I'm thankful to the Lord for it," Owens says gracefully. "Maybe I was just the right guy to be used at the right time. I just thank the Lord that I was used in that situation. Now, when I watch Auburn, I can see all the changes that have come. It makes me feel good."

In fact, Walls was called on to be a blocker on every running play, which meant almost every play. "My responsibility was the first person who showed up on the inside. It was usually the inside linebacker or defensive end," Walls says. "All I needed to do was make a good lick and hold it for a second. I never minded that."

It took a remarkable set of circumstances for Walls to have an opportunity to be Auburn's starting quarterback. First, Dieter Brock, who would later rewrite the Canadian Football League passing record book, left for Jacksonville State when Ted Smith was moved ahead of him during the 1971 season. When Lyons was injured, Smith, Walls, and Wade Whatley remained. "About three days before A-Day, Lyons hurt his knee," recalls Walls. "I just had a better spring game than the rest of them. If Lyons hadn't been hurt, I probably wouldn't have ever taken a snap."

The 1972 season started with a 14–3 win over Mississippi State on a hot day in Jackson. A week later, Auburn barely got past UT-Chattanooga 14–7. The defense had to turn away a late threat to avoid what would have been one of the more embarrassing losses in school history. The pundits, it seemed, had been right. If Auburn had to struggle to beat the Moccasins, what would happen against Tennessee the following week in Birmingham?

What happened was, Auburn found a way. Henley ran eleven consecutive times between the tackles on a 16-play, 81-yard touchdown drive. Walls threw just one pass all day. When Gardner Jett kicked a 30-yard field goal to make it 10–0 in the third quarter, it was as good as over. The defense wasn't about to let Tennessee score twice.

A week later, Auburn held on to beat Ole Miss 19–13 in Jackson. The nation began to take notice. But on October 14 in

The Call

Recordings are still played today of play-by-play announcer Gary Sanders's call of the most memorable play in Auburn history on December 2, 1972. It went like this:

Here we go. Fourth down and nine yards to go for the University of Alabama. Deep is Johnny Simmons. That means David Langner is up on the line of scrimmage again. Langner will be on the far right, Roger Mitchell on the left. Auburn is again going after the kick as you might imagine. Greg Gantt is standing on his own 30. Auburn will try to block it. Auburn is going after it. Here's a good snap. It is blocked! It is blocked! It's caught on the run! It's caught on the run, he's gonna score! David Langner! David Langner has scored and Auburn has tied the game! Roger Mitchell blocked the kick! Roger Mitchell blocked the kick and it's 16–16! The entire Auburn team has come out to get David Langner!

Baton Rouge, the magic seemed to run out. In a battle of the unbeatens, LSU romped to a 35–7 victory before a record Tiger Stadium crowd of 70,000. Back home against Georgia Tech, Auburn players seemed listless. The Yellow Jackets jumped to a 14–0 lead. Auburn brought it up to 14–10 in the fourth quarter. Walls scored on a 1-yard sneak; after Beck returned an interception 35 yards, Walls hit Gossom on an 8-yard touchdown pass, and the Tigers had done it again, winning 24–14.

Week after week, the Tigers did just enough, defying the odds so often that *Birmingham News* columnist Clyde Bolton dubbed them "The Amazin's." They led Florida State 27–0 and cruised home 27–14, intercepting passing whiz Gary Huff four times. They led 26–0 at Florida and fought off a frantic Gator rally to win 26–20. Henley was injured and couldn't play against Georgia, but sophomore Chris Linderman scored twice and the Tigers earned their most lopsided win of the season, 27–10.

Meanwhile, Alabama was destroying opponent after opponent. After two straight six-win seasons, Bryant had gone to the wishbone offense. He unveiled it in the opener at Southern California, and the Tide pulled a 17–3 upset. Except for a 17–10 loss at Tennessee, the Alabama juggernaut never slowed.

Auburn went into the annual showdown at Legion Field with an 8–1 record, ranked number nine in the nation and headed for the Gator Bowl, but few expected the Cinderella story to continue. Alabama was 10–0 and ranked number two. The Tide had its eyes on a national championship. Most thought the Alabama offensive line, anchored by future Hall of Famer John Hannah, would pulverize the Auburn defense, giving shifty quarterback Terry Davis ample room to operate.

The Tide had more than a powerful offense. Its defense was among the best in the land. Auburn's mostly one-dimensional offense faced its biggest challenge of the season. The Tide, which would play Texas in the Cotton Bowl, was a 16-point favorite. In the two-week break before the game, Bryant made a statement he would regret. "I'd rather beat the cow college than beat Texas ten times," he told the Birmingham Quarterback Club. Auburn fans seethed. Henley, ever outspoken, spoke for them all. "I think it's low down for a coach sixty years old to call our school a cow college," Henley said. "I'm speaking up for Auburn."

Auburn gained just 81 yards total offense against Alabama. With Newton leading the way, the defense fought into the fourth quarter. But Alabama was firmly in control. Few thought the extra point Roger Mitchell had blocked in the first half would matter. Fewer still noticed that Auburn seemingly was on the verge of blocking almost every punt. The Tigers finally got close enough for Jordan to send Jett in to try a 44-yard field goal. Auburn fans booed. Alabama fans booed, too, believing Jordan was simply trying to avoid a shutout.

Bobby Davis was a sophomore linebacker watching from the sidelines. He wondered what Jordan was thinking. "The folks on the sideline had pretty well given up the ship," Davis says. "Coach Jordan gets ready to kick a field goal. We are saying 'The old man has finally lost his mind.' Of course, it was the smartest thing he ever did."

On his weekly television show, even Bryant chastised those who booed when Jordan went for the field goal. "Shug Jordan's not an idiot. He knew that was the right thing to do." Jett made the kick, which equaled the longest of his career, to make the score 16–3 with 9:15 left in the game. There was no celebration in the stands or on the Auburn sideline. Little did Jett know just how much that field goal would mean.

The crowd of 72,386 was about to see a miracle unfold. With 5:30 left in the game, Greg Gantt dropped back to punt. Newton broke free at the line of scrimmage and blocked it. The ball

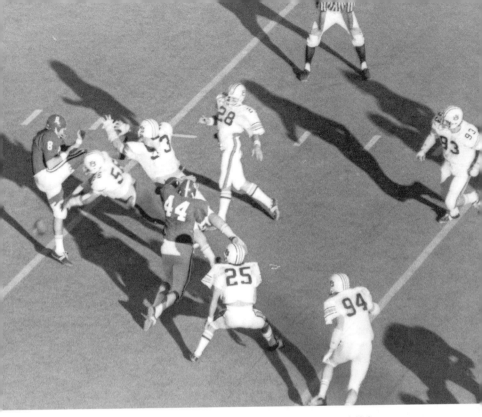

The first blocked punt in the 1972 showdown between Auburn and Alabama.

bounced high off the artificial turf into the waiting arms of Langner, who ran untouched into the end zone. An official, for some reason, dropped his hat where Langner picked up the ball. After a brief discussion, it was ruled a touchdown. Holder Dave Beck got an errant snap on the tee, and Jett kicked the extra point to make it 16–10.

At least Auburn would leave with some pride. The score would be close, even if the game had not been. That was the thinking as Alabama awaited the kickoff. The Tide stayed conservative, content to run the ball and drain the clock, and picked up two first downs. One more, and the game would be over. Mike Neel gave

Auburn a sliver of hope when he knifed through to tackle Alabama quarterback Terry Davis for a loss on third down. Auburn called time-out. Alabama would have to punt one more time.

On the Alabama sideline, the belief was that the rush had come from the outside on the prior blocked punt. Gantt was told to move two steps closer to the line of scrimmage, making the angle more difficult for outside rushers. Bad idea. Newton lined up on the guard's outside shoulder, having moved down from his normal position on the tackle's outside shoulder. Alabama's line did not respond. "I never expected it to happen or not to happen," Newton says. "I knew we'd put some good rushes on their punter all day long."

Instant replay: the second blocked punt.

Then the ball was snapped.

"The guard just kind of glanced at me," Newton says. "It opened up. I could see the upback was blocking somebody else. I just timed my steps to get in front of the ball."

In a scene that will live in Auburn glory and Alabama infamy, Newton blocked Gantt's punt again. Amazingly, the ball again hopped high off the turf and once more into Langner's arms. He took it home with 1:34 left. Auburn's bench emptied as players mobbed Langner in the end zone. Jett kicked the extra point, and Auburn was ahead 17–16. Fittingly, Langner put the exclamation point on it all when he intercepted Davis's desperation pass to kill Alabama's last hope.

Newton will forever be remembered as the man who blocked the two punts. But there may never have been an Auburn linebacker who played better against the Tide. He was in on 23 tackles, roaming from sideline to sideline. Without him, Auburn might not have been close enough for two blocked punts to matter. When it was over, Auburn players celebrated loud and long in their Legion Field locker room. Just a few feet away, Alabama players sat in stunned silence. "When those cows get mad, they kick," Henley said wryly. "I know, because I've been around 'em all my life. There won't be enough people back in Auburn to milk 'em tonight."

Back in Auburn, Toomer's Corner, where Auburn students traditionally celebrate victories by throwing streams of toilet tissue into the trees, was bathed in white. "Punt, Bama, Punt" became a joyful Auburn cry for the ages. Now, more than three decades later, no Auburn victory has been sweeter or more memorable. It is unlikely one ever will be. It was the signature game

Five More Shockers

Auburn 27, number-one ranked Georgia 13: On November 21, 1942, Auburn earned what was then the most significant victory in school history. Georgia was unbeaten and ranked first. Auburn was 4-4-1. Florida had beaten Auburn 6-0, and Georgia had beaten Florida 72-0. Halfback Monk Gafford outplayed Georgia Heisman Trophy winner Frank Sinkwich, rushing for 119 yards on 20 carries and 3 punts for 92 yards.

Auburn 14, Alabama 13: Auburn and Alabama had played in 1948 for the first time since 1907, and the Tigers had been embarrassed 55-0. On December 3, 1949, more of the same was expected. Auburn was 1-4-3. Alabama was 6-2-1. Behind spectacular quarterback Travis Tidwell, Auburn took a 14-7 lead in the fourth quarter. Alabama's Tom Calvin scored to make it 14-13, but Ed Salem missed the extra point.

Auburn 24, Vanderbilt 14: In Ralph Jordan's first game as head coach on September 29, 1951, Auburn made a statement that times had changed. Auburn had been 0-10 in 1950, and Vanderbilt, led by quarterback Bill Wade, was supposed to win easily. Instead, the Tigers took control early and gave Jordan a welcome home present at Cliff Hare Stadium

Auburn 36, number-one ranked Florida 33: Auburn had won sixteen straight games, but the powerful Gators were 17–point favorites at the Swamp in Gainesville on October 15, 1994. Patrick Nix threw an 8-yard touchdown pass to Frank Sanders in the final seconds as the Tigers knocked off the Gators for the second consecutive season.

Auburn 23, number-one ranked Florida 20: On October 13, 2001, at Jordan-Hare Stadium, quarterback Daniel Cox came off the bench as Auburn once again cost Florida its perch atop the polls. Damon Duval's field goal with ten seconds left gave the Gators their first loss of the season.

Auburn players are jubilant following their 1972 win over Alabama.

in a remarkable Auburn season. "The game was so significant and the setting was so extraordinary," Newton says. "Everybody was waiting for our wheels to run off. Nobody believed we could win, but we never doubted it."

In the Gator Bowl, Auburn had to earn respect again. Walls was injured in practice and replaced by Whatley. Colorado was a substantial favorite. At the annual Gator Bowl banquet, Colorado players taunted Auburn players. The Tigers romped to a 24–3 victory, and Whatley was named the game's most valuable player. Auburn finished 10–1 and ranked fifth in the Associated Press poll. It missed out on a share of the Southeastern Conference championship only because Alabama played one more SEC game.

But for all the remarkable accomplishments of the 1972 team, it was the win over Alabama that will live always in Auburn football lore. When the game was over, as the crowd screamed outside, an emotional Jordan paid his highest compliment to the men around him. "In twenty-two years I have always hesitated to put one of my teams ahead of any of the others, but today I'm putting this team at the top of the list," said a beaming Jordan.

Jordan retired three years later, and it was ten long, painful years before Auburn beat Alabama again. But the men who made it happen, most now in their fifties, are still proud today. They weren't the biggest, fastest, or most talented team on the field that day. They were just the best. They believed it before the game. And they believe it today. "I never expected anything but that we would win," Newton says.

In Hamilton, Alabama, Bill's oldest brother, Joe, worked that year at a mobile home plant. A former Auburn basketball player, Joe had a running debate going with coworkers of the Alabama persuasion. Bill remembers, "He called me and said 'Can y'all beat 'em?' I told him to bet the house."

The
Transformation

As Christmas season arrived in 1980, Pat Dye watched the events unfolding far to the east with growing interest. Georgia, Dye's alma mater, would play for the national championship against Notre Dame in the Sugar Bowl. It was a poorly kept secret that Bulldog coach Vince Dooley was having serious talks with Auburn, his alma mater, where luckless Doug Barfield had resigned under pressure after five seasons.

Dye, who had been an All-American as an undersized Georgia lineman, was a hot coaching prospect. His name was mentioned in connection with virtually every job that came open. He was ready to pounce if Dooley bolted for Auburn. If Dooley stayed at Georgia, Dye wanted to go to Auburn. Just as he was about to sign an Auburn contract, Dooley hesitated. He couldn't bring himself to do it. He stayed at Georgia and went on to lead the Bulldogs to a 17–10 victory over Notre Dame and the national championship. "If I'd been ten years younger, I'd have jumped across the Chattahoochee River to go back to Auburn," Dooley recollects, "but we just decided we had too much invested in Georgia to leave." Auburn officials, caught by surprise, began their search anew. Dye quickly emerged as a leading candidate, but he wasn't the only candidate. Auburn officials moved deliberately.

At Wyoming Dye was under pressure to sign a contract extension. Finally, he was given an ultimatum: Sign the contract or resign. He resigned, unsure if he would get an offer from Auburn. Finally, in early January, the call came. Dye was appointed Auburn's head football coach. Dye had attracted attention as a hard-nosed linebackers coach for Alabama coach Bear Bryant. He'd gone 48–18–1 in six seasons at East Carolina before going to Wyoming. And now he was back in the Southeastern Conference, turning a deaf ear to Bryant's recommendation that he not take the Auburn job.

Auburn football has never been the same. Today tickets are scarce at Jordan-Hare Stadium, and often sold out. Auburn's facilities are among the nation's best, its coaches among the higher paid. Athletes from coast to coast listen when Auburn calls. When Dye arrived at Auburn, he found a program low on talent and lower on spirit. Auburn had lost eight straight to Alabama, and there appeared to be no relief in sight. But Dye made it clear from the start that he would back away from no one.

Asked how long it would take him to beat Alabama, Dye didn't flinch. "Sixty minutes," he said. Dye won an SEC championship in 1983, and he won three straight between 1987 and 1989. He would make Auburn football great again, like it had been in the glory days of Shug Jordan.

Randy Campbell, who at 5'11" and 165 pounds parlayed toughness and smarts into becoming a two-year starter at quarterback in Auburn's wishbone offense, remembers the first day he and his teammates met their new coach. They were accustomed to Barfield's laidback ways. It took only minutes for them to realize things had changed. "The first impression was the first team meeting we had," Campbell recalls. "He threw two guys out of the meeting because they weren't paying attention. He basically proceeded to tell us that he'd won championships at every level. He said he knew how to win and that we were going to win. He said, most of all, we weren't going to fear Alabama. That got my attention. He came across very, very confident. We kind of walked out of there and said, 'He's really the right guy and things are going to get real good real quick or he's full of it.' The forty who thought he was full of it weren't there very long."

Winning, Dye told his players, would come only at a high price. He drove that point home long before he coached his first game. "That winter and spring training was the hardest thing I've ever been through," Campbell reminisces. "There were three phases to the winter program. Phase 1, we thought, was kind of a joke. We lifted hard, but we were used to doing that." Phase 2,

Pat Dye expected— and got—the best out of his Auburn players.

held in the old inflatable "bubble" that was once Auburn's indoor practice facility, was no joke. "The first day of Phase 2, some of the guys in our group were walking to the bubble," Campbell says. "Here came four guys holding Darryl Wilkes up, bringing him out. He was a free safety. He was about 6'2", 175 pounds, and one of the best athletes on the team. He was soaking wet and about to pass out. That was Phase 2. We don't even want to talk about Phase 3, but it got real hard, real quick."

It was so hard that players welcomed spring practice, but they found out that wasn't going to be any easier. "I can remember players being so tired coaches would hold them up at the line of scrimmage," Campbell says. "When the ball was snapped, they'd shove them in there. We were just trying to find out who was tough and who wasn't. Between thirty and forty people left the program."

Those who remained were fiercely proud and are fiercely proud today. They grew as close as brothers, armed with the belief that after what they had gone through, they could withstand anything. The 1981 Tigers were 5–6, but they played with ferocity and toughness that made it clear that the bad times would soon be over. Alabama beat Auburn for the ninth straight time, 28–17, on the day Bryant broke Amos Alonzo Stagg's record for victories, but the Tigers led in the fourth quarter.

"If we'd done a better job of coaching, we'd have had a chance to win three more games," Dye says. "We should have beaten Mississippi State and Tennessee. We did beat Wake Forest. They just stole that game from us. When you look back, if we'd won eight games that year we might have gotten a false sense of who we were. We might not have accomplished what we did later."

When the season was over, Dye and his staff turned their attention to what would be their first full recruiting class. The Tigers had won just five games, but the way they'd played and Dye's fierce belief in himself and his program had attracted attention. Parade All-America running back Alan Evans of Enterprise, the state's top prospect, signed on. Tommie Agee, who would become one of Auburn's all-time great fullbacks, had grown up in Maplesville as an Alabama fan. He signed with Auburn. But the recruit who would become an American sports icon came from Bessemer. He played football, baseball, and ran track at McAdory High School, a half-hour drive from the University of Alabama campus. He'd played mostly defense in high school, running the ball fewer than a dozen times a game. His name was Vincent Jackson. His friends called him Bo.

Auburn secondary coach Bobby Wallace, who recruited the Birmingham area, got Jackson away from Alabama, his lifelong favorite. It didn't hurt that Alabama assistant Ken Donahue told Jackson that he "might" start by the time he was a junior. Jackson signed with Auburn, turning down a $250,000 signing bonus from the New York Yankees, and reported to campus for the 1982 season. By the time he left after the 1985 season, he had won the Heisman Trophy and had become the greatest running back in Auburn history. "You could tell he was different," remarks Campbell. "He was bigger and stronger than anybody we had who wasn't a lineman. He was faster than anybody, period." There was no jealousy among the upperclassmen, however. They could see this guy was something different. "The thing is, he was so much better than everybody," Campbell says. "Nobody went back to their rooms saying 'I can't believe they put that freshman ahead of me.' It was like if I was playing quarterback and all of a sudden John Elway had transferred to Auburn. It was that obvious."

Jackson was key, but there were others. When Jack Crowe arrived to replace Alex Gibbs as offensive coordinator in 1982, he identified Campbell, who had played some wide receiver in 1981, as one who could be a winning wishbone quarterback. Lionel "Little Train" James was a devastating blocker and dangerous runner who became one of Auburn's more popular players ever. Steve Wallace played left tackle on his way to a Hall of Fame career in the NFL. Tight ends Jeff Parks and Ed West were headed for the NFL. Outside linebacker Kevin Greene was going from walk-on to star and would eventually be a great pass rusher in the NFL. Gregg Carr, who had come from Woodlawn to play for Barfield, was on his way to becoming an All-America linebacker.

Wayne Hall, the line coach who became defensive coordinator after the 1985 season, began what would become a tradition of sending players to the NFL. So grateful were those linemen that, years later, they got together to buy him a Rolex watch. Carr, who walked away from a promising NFL career to become an orthopedist, says, "I think my recruiting class was ranked ninth out of ten classes in the SEC. About half the kids quit. The kids that remained formed the backbone of those later Auburn teams. I think we had eight or nine guys play professional football. When Dye came in there, he worked us like animals. He got more out of us than we thought we were capable of producing. That's why he was a great coach. Coach Dye wanted young, hungry guys he could build a program around."

On September 25, 1982, the Tigers signaled they would be a force to be reckoned with. They beat Tennessee 24–14 at Jordan-

Doug's Disappointment

It was the opportunity for which Doug Barfield had worked for all of his adult life. In spring 1975, when legendary coach Shug Jordan announced he would retire at the end of the next season, Auburn president Harry Philpott anointed Barfield as Auburn's next coach. Barfield, the offensive coordinator who had installed Auburn's veer offense, was not the unanimous choice. Jordan and many Auburn people wanted defensive coordinator Paul Davis. The house was divided. To make it more difficult, Auburn was coming off a ten-win season and most thought the future looked bright.

Barfield and Jordan knew better. The talent level had fallen. The football program began to flounder, and anger turned to bitterness. Auburn won just three games in 1975. The program Barfield inherited was woefully short of SEC caliber players. NCAA probation would come three years later. Through it all, Barfield rebuilt the talent level and won games. He won three games in 1976, five in 1977, six in

Hare Stadium to run their record to 3–0 and climb to number twenty in the polls. "It was our biggest game and our biggest win since I've been here," Dye said when it was over. "This was a game we wanted very badly. We had to have it if we were going to compete on a national level."

There was a step back the following week when Nebraska came to town. The mighty Cornhuskers were much too strong

1978, and eight in 1979. He beat Georgia. He beat Florida. He beat Tennessee. But beating Alabama and Bear Bryant was too much. He was 0–5.

Barfield was 29–25 in five seasons, not bad considering where he started. It wasn't enough to win the hearts of Auburn people. The Tigers were supposed to be good in 1980, but they lost 42–0 to Tennessee before a sellout crowd at Jordan-Hare Stadium. For Barfield, it was as good as over. His team limped home 5–6.

Barfield made the best deal he could and was gone. Pat Dye won an SEC championship three years later with a team built around Barfield's recruits. "It was a difficult time," Barfield recalls, "but that was a long time ago." He won't go much deeper than that.

Barfield's ego never swelled, nor did his bank account. He made $48,000 in his final season at Auburn. "People don't believe me when I tell them what I made then," Barfield says. "I would have coached for groceries."

and romped to a 41–7 victory. But Auburn's march was only interrupted. It would not stop. Auburn also lost a disputed 19–17 decision to Florida in Gainesville and almost pulled off a huge upset before falling to number-one-ranked Georgia 19–14 in one of the more memorable games ever played at Jordan-Hare Stadium.

But it was on November 27 at Birmingham's Legion Field that Auburn football turned the corner, and Auburn fans knew beyond question that they had the right man as their coach. The Tigers rallied from a 22–14 deficit in the fourth quarter to beat Alabama 23–22. Jackson scored the winning touchdown from the 1 yard line on fourth down. To this day, the phrase "Bo over the top" needs no explanation to any Auburn fan anywhere. Ten long years of frustration and humiliation were over. Auburn fans stormed the field, tearing down the goal posts at both ends. Auburn players returned from the locker room to join the celebration. It was the last Iron Bowl for Bryant, who announced his retirement weeks later and died a month after coaching his last game in the Liberty Bowl. The Tigers beat Boston College and Doug Flutie 33–28 in the Tangerine Bowl and turned their attention toward the future. They had proved they were good. The next step was to be great.

Great they were in 1983, but the journey was hard. On a hot August afternoon in 1983, coaches and players wept together, consoling one another and dealing with overwhelming grief. Fullback Greg Pratt had collapsed after making his required time in running tests and died a short time later. Dye calls it the most difficult day of his coaching career. "There's no way to describe what it was like going through that," Dye recalls. "We went through the practices, but it was like a funeral. The kids worked anyway, and the coaches got them through it." From those days of grief, Auburn's football team began to grow. It became one of the more dominant teams ever to play at Jordan-Hare Stadium, going 11–1 and winning the SEC championship.

It was in Athens, however, where Dye had reached greatness as a player, that Auburn claimed a long-coveted championship and Sugar Bowl bid with a 13–7 victory over unbeaten Georgia.

In the locker room, Dye licked sugar off a football: "God almighty, that was a great day," he says. "Winning the SEC championship, doing it at Georgia. That meant a lot to a lot of people." Those who played and those who coached believe to this day they should have been national champions.

Auburn lost 20–7 to Texas in the second game of the season, then won ten straight against one of the tougher schedules in college football history. On January 1, Nebraska and Texas, both unbeaten, were 1–2 in the polls. Auburn was third, Georgia fourth, and Miami fifth. In the afternoon, Georgia knocked off Texas in the Cotton Bowl. As Auburn and number-eight-ranked Michigan battled in the Sugar Bowl, Miami beat Nebraska in the Orange Bowl. When Al Del Greco trotted out to kick what would be the game-winning field goal in Auburn's 9–7 victory, he thought he was kicking for the national championship. But when the polls came out the next day, Miami had jumped from fifth to first. Nebraska was second and Auburn was still third. "We won the national championship," says Joe Whitt, who has been an Auburn assistant since joining Dye in 1981. "They didn't give it to us, but we won it. I'll always feel like we were national champions." National champion or not, Auburn was once again a major player in college football. Dye had shown the way to the first SEC championship since 1957 and the first eleven-win season in school history. More days of glory were ahead, but first the Tigers would be humbled.

They were ranked number one in the preseason polls in 1984, only to lose to Miami in the Kickoff Classic and at Texas, which made them 0–2. They were heavily favored over a four-win Alabama team but lost 17–15. In 1985 they climbed back to

Pat Dye makes a point at a press conference.

the top two weeks into the season but lost to Tennessee and Florida before falling again to Alabama, this time on Van Tiffin's 53-yard field goal as time expired. They were blitzed 36–16 by Texas A&M in the Cotton Bowl. Jackson won the Heisman Trophy, but for the first time, there was some grumbling about the coaching and the direction of the program. By the end of 1986, those questions had been answered. The Tigers went 10–2, beating Alabama 21–17 on Lawyer Tillman's reverse in the final minute. They beat Southern California 16–7 in the Florida Citrus Bowl and finished sixth in the polls.

The 1987 season started a run of three straight SEC championships and two more trips to the Sugar Bowl. A steady stream of players went from Auburn to the NFL. The Tigers won four straight from Alabama. In 1988 Tracy Rocker won the Lombardi Trophy as the nation's top defensive player and the Outland Award as the nation's top lineman.

Perhaps the signature of Dye's time at Auburn will always be December 2, 1989. That was the day Alabama visited Jordan-Hare Stadium for the first time. It was a moment many Auburn people thought would never come, but Dye would not rest until it did. In surely the most emotional Auburn football game ever played, the Tigers knocked off unbeaten Alabama 30–20 to earn a share of their third straight SEC championship.

Dye built a powerhouse on his beliefs of hard work and physical play. He believed football is a test of will, of endurance, of willingness to sacrifice. He is still skeptical today of pass-oriented, spread offenses. "You can do all that stuff, but you win the game the old Coach Bryant way, the old Coach Jordan way," Dye says. "You win it with defense, not turning the ball over, and playing smart."

Dye changed the culture of football in Alabama. He came along at an advantageous time, just as Bryant was stepping down at Alabama. Suddenly, Alabama was no longer the automatic place to go for the top players in the state. Ben Tamburello, who would become an All-America center, grew up an Alabama fan, but he enrolled at Auburn for winter quarter in 1983. He was there for the championship season of 1983 and was a key player in the turnaround season of 1986.

"So many things were changing with Coach Bryant and his career," Tamburello remembers. "You could see the way the pendulum was turning. I took my visit the week of the Alabama game. I was able to see how they prepared and to talk to Coach Dye. I'd just been at Alabama a few weeks before that. Sitting around and talking to Coach Dye, seeing the way they prepared, seeing some of the players and the relationships they had with each other, it was obvious it was a really special place."

It was a decision, Tamburello says, that is still paying dividends today. "I think my decision to go play for Coach Dye was the best one I ever made," Tamburello says. "The reason I went there was to get my education, play on a championship team, and build a platform where I could go on to a successful life. We didn't win a national championship, but it couldn't have worked out any better."

Ben Thomas "grew up" with Dye. He was a freshman on Dye's first team, a lightly recruited defensive tackle who went on to a productive career in the NFL. "You had different guys from different places, from different backgrounds that believed in different things" Thomas says. "What made us win was we believed in each other and we believed in our head coach and his staff. Whatever they said, we believed. We played very hard. That's the way we were taught. We had to outlast anybody we played. That's how we prepared ourselves. We knew what Coach Dye expected of us and we did those things."

It didn't end the way Dye wanted it to end. The program sagged after 1989. There was an 8–3–1 record in 1990. In 1991 former defensive back Eric Ramsey, accused of receiving improper payments from an Auburn assistant coach, sparked an investigation that ultimately landed Auburn on NCAA probation. The 1991 Tigers went 5–6. They were 5–5–1 in 1992. "We got fat and sassy and I did a poor job of coaching," Dye admits. "We started down in 1990. We had the thing on the way back in 1992. We struggled and came awfully close to being a good team."

Dye, who was not mentioned in the findings, nevertheless announced his resignation on Thanksgiving night, less than twenty-four hours before the Iron Bowl. His players walked into the stadium with helmets held high in a silent salute, but they were no match for an Alabama team on its way to the national championship, and the Tigers lost 17–0.

"If there is anything people can learn from me, it is that there is a blessing in all things," says Dye, who was 99–39–4 at Auburn. "Life isn't always fair. What you have to do is find the blessing. That's what I've done. I don't have any regrets." Nothing that happened in the early 1990s could change what had happened in the decade before. Dye had delivered on every promise. Auburn football had been transformed.

A Day for Rejoicing

The brick occupies a prominent place in the office of former Auburn athletics director David Housel. The inscription reads: THE FINAL BRICK. DECEMBER 2, 1989, JORDAN-HARE STADIUM. AUBURN 30, ALABAMA 20. It is a powerful symbol of triumph for Auburn people everywhere. For four decades, Auburn fans felt outnumbered and unwelcome when they played Alabama at Birmingham's Legion Field. Finally, on that memorable day in 1989, the Crimson Tide came to their house.

It was a day that athletics director Jeff Beard and football coach Shug Jordan had talked about when they began in the early 1950s to build a program. Beard lived to see it. Jordan did not.

"That's the final brick in the dream Coach Jordan and Coach Beard had dating back to when they were Auburn athletes in the late '20s and early '30s," Housel says. "It was a dream not just of getting Alabama here, but the dream of having a facility big enough, good enough, and fine enough and a program big enough, good enough, and fine enough that all our conference brothers would come here and play. We wouldn't have to play Georgia Tech in Atlanta and Birmingham. We wouldn't have to play Tennessee in Birmingham. We wouldn't have to go to Columbus to play Georgia. We wouldn't have to go to Birmingham to play the Crimson Tide. They would come to our house."

Georgia played at Auburn for the first time in 1960. Georgia Tech, no longer a regular opponent but once a bitter rival, came to town in 1971, and Tennessee in 1974. In all those years the Alabama game was played in Birmingham, the tickets being divided evenly between the two schools. But the crowd rarely seemed to be even. "Having the game in Auburn gives Auburn a home-field advantage it never had in Birmingham," Housel says. "Truth, like beauty is in the eye of the beholder. For whatever reason, right or wrong, Auburn people always thought Alabama had a home-field advantage. Most Auburn people thought Legion Field was as neutral as the beaches of Normandy on D-Day."

Glen Gulledge, owner of Byron's Smokehouse, an immensely popular Auburn restaurant, says that "When you walk in that gate and there is a bronze monument of Bear Bryant, you sure don't feel like you are the home team." No team ever had more of a home-field advantage than Auburn the first time Alabama came to town. Joe Whitt, an Auburn assistant coach since 1981, smiles at the memory. "Loud? It was unbelievable. I don't know if anybody can ever outdo that. I was on the sideline, and you couldn't hear the guy from the press box on the headphones. You couldn't hear the guy next to you. It was amazing."

It was a day many Auburn people thought they'd never see. Jordan, who retired as head coach after the 1975 season, was once asked if Auburn's home game against Alabama would ever be moved to Jordan-Hare. "There'll have to be some prominent funerals," he said. But, by the mid-1980s, the landscape had changed. Dye had made Auburn a Southeastern Conference power. Jordan-Hare Stadium was being enlarged to seat more than 85,000. Every other SEC team could play its home games where it wanted. Why not Auburn?

Alabama athletic director Steve Sloan made the mistake of seeming to have sympathy for Auburn's position. "When you get down to it, the home team really has the right to choose where to play its home game," Sloan says. "It's almost indefensible to say someone can't do that, unless there are contractual obligations that say otherwise." The Alabama position was that it had a contract to play Auburn at Legion Field through 1992. So contentious was the debate that then Alabama president, Joab Thomas, even suggested in a letter to then Auburn president, James Martin, that the two teams stop playing on an annual basis.

Alabama coach Ray Perkins, who left for the Tampa Bay Bucs after the 1986 season, was adamantly opposed to going where Alabama had never been before. "It won't happen," Perkins stated. But it did. "There wasn't anything to keep us playing the game in

Auburn," says Dye. "We had as many seats as they had in Birmingham. As a matter of fact, by the time we played the game, we had more seats than they had in Birmingham. Everything about playing the game in Auburn and going home and home with Alabama rather than splitting the tickets was a plus for Auburn and Alabama. Alabama didn't want to admit it at the time."

Trustees Bobby Lowder, Morris Savage, and Mike McCartney were given the responsibility of representing Auburn in negotiations. Ultimately, it came down to talks between Lowder for Auburn and Winton "Red" Blount for Alabama. Later, Lowder said, "Alabama fought us and fought us. They had some sort of contract they claimed Bear Bryant had signed and everything else that ran through 1992. We met with them and pretty well said 'We're going to play the 1989 game in Auburn.' They sure didn't want to play there. They were pretty hostile. It didn't make sense to me. What I said from the very beginning is it is our home game and we can play it wherever we want to."

Finally, a deal was reached. The 50–50 ticket split at Legion Field, the practice since 1948, would be changed, and Alabama would have the home team's share of tickets in 1988. The game would go to Auburn in 1989. Auburn's concession was to play one more home game against Alabama in Birmingham in 1991. "We didn't want to go to court over that contract," Lowder says. "They had a contract that was signed by Coach Bryant and supposedly signed by [former Auburn athletic director] Lee Hayley. We really questioned that it was a valid contract, but to go to court, we didn't think it was worth it."

The deal was done. The buildup was immense as the game approached. Alabama was 10–0 and ranked number two in the nation. Auburn was 8–2, having lost close games at Tennessee and Florida State. Alabama could win the SEC championship outright with a victory and hold on to hope for a national championship. Auburn, which had won the previous two titles, could make it a three-way tie with Alabama and Tennessee.

Fans began to arrive early in the week. At game time, thousands were outside the stadium, unable to get tickets. The noise was deafening from the start and never abated. It was the most memorable day of Dye's coaching career. "Oh, hell yeah," he remembers. "Nobody could predict the emotions of that day. It would have been impossible. There's never been one like that before and there hasn't been one like that since. There never will be, because we won't ever have that kind of occasion again. I never had any doubt we were going to win the game."

As game day neared, emotions ran high on both sides. Alabama was a slight favorite, and Auburn fans worried that the day for which they had waited for so long would be spoiled by an Alabama victory. When polled by the Associated Press, twenty of twenty-four state sportswriters predicted the Crimson Tide would win. "All those things are fine," Dye said the week before the game, "but the most significant thing about the game is it's in Auburn. It's going to be a great occasion. The fact that Alabama is undefeated and we have a chance to share our third straight SEC championship makes it even more significant. Those things won't increase the intensity, but they add to the importance of the first Auburn-Alabama game to be played at Jordan-Hare Stadium."

Alabama coach Bill Curry poured fuel on the fire when he went public with what he claimed were threatening letters to players. He even informed the FBI. Bill Beckwith, the late

Auburn quarterback Reggie
Slack takes the snap.

Auburn athletic business manager, retorted that didn't want "riff-raff" from Alabama hanging around outside the stadium during the game. Finally, it was time to play.

Tiger Walk, the traditional trek by Auburn players and coaches to the stadium, was a madhouse. A record crowd of 85,319 filled the stadium. Thousands more milled around outside. "There is no way to describe how this football team felt coming down to the stadium today with all the people lining the street," Dye said after Auburn had won. "I tried to stay out of the way, but seeing the looks in the faces of Auburn people must have been like the Berlin Wall coming down. It was as if they were freed and came out of bondage. I didn't know what it would do to the players. I made a concerted effort to calm them down. They were as high as I've ever seen. James Joseph is as tough as they come, but he hyperventilated before we came on the field."

If they didn't know already, Alabama players and coaches saw what they were up against as they arrived. Fans rocked their buses, banging on the windows as they went past. Jim Fuller, now the athletics director at Jacksonville State University, was Alabama's offensive line coach. "I've said many times that on that day, in that game, Auburn was going to win," Fuller says. "I didn't have that feeling before the game, but during the course of the game, I did. That was Auburn's day. It was a first. It was a big event. It was something they'd been looking forward to for a long time."

For Curry, it was another in a long line of disappointments against Auburn. Curry had been 0–6 against Auburn at Georgia Tech. He left that day 0–4 against Auburn at Alabama. Never really accepted by Alabama fans, Curry left for Kentucky just over a month later.

Auburn moved quickly to take the lead, scoring on its first possession when James Joseph went in from the 1 yard line. Alabama made it 7–3 on a 24-yard Philip Doyle field goal. Gary Hollingsworth's 18-yard pass to Marco Battle and Doyle's extra point gave the Tide a 10–7 halftime lead. But Auburn wasn't going to be denied, not this day. Though they were behind, a play early in the third quarter told Auburn players they had the upper hand. Alabama took the kickoff and went to Auburn's 30-yard line in six plays. Instead of running for the first down, Hollingsworth tried to pass. It was incomplete. "We expected Alabama to play smashmouth football," outside linebacker Craig Ogletree said, a hint of disdain in his voice. Dye added, "I always like it when people throw on third-and-one."

Joseph ran 2 yards for a touchdown in the third quarter. Lyle's extra point made it 14–10, and Auburn was in command. Lyle kicked a 22-yard field goal to make it 17–10, and Lectron Williams ran 12 yards for another touchdown. Lyle kicked the extra point, and a 31-yard field goal to make it 27–10.

Alabama wasn't unbeaten by accident. The Tide fought back. Hollingsworth threw a 15-yard touchdown pass to Battle, and Doyle's extra point made it 27–17. Doyle kicked a 23-yard field goal, putting Alabama in striking distance at 27–20. But as the hour grew late, Lyle kicked a 34-yarder to make it 30–20. The celebration began.

Quarterback Reggie Slack completed 14 of 26 passes for 274 yards for Auburn. Alexander Wright, a wide receiver with world-class speed, caught seven of those passes for 141 yards. Stacy Danley rushed 35 times for 130 yards. "Our game plan was to be freewheeling," Slack said as his teammates celebrated around

Slack Torches Tide

Reggie Slack did all sorts of good things as Auburn's starting quarterback. He had a record of 22–4 as a starter. With 4,697 yards, he is the number-six passer in Auburn history. He led the Tigers to two consecutive Southeastern Conference championships. On December 2, 1989, he was at his best. Slack completed 14 of 26 passes for 274 yards in leading the Tigers to a 30–20 victory.

Seven of Slack's passes went to speedy Alexander Wright for 141 yards. Not bad for a day's work for one who wasn't even sure he would be a quarterback when arrived at Auburn.

Assistant coach Joe Whitt recruited Slack out of Milton, Florida. "To be honest, I just knew he was a good person," Whitt notes. "I'd watched him since the eighth grade, watched him play football since the tenth grade. I knew he had a good chance to be a good player at some position. I appealed to Coach Dye, 'Coach, let me have him at linebacker.' We signed him as an athlete. Coach Dye came in the locker room after the very first practice. He kind of smiled and said 'You're not going to see him at linebacker.'"

him. "We felt like we had to be. With the potential Alabama had to score, we knew we had to put points on the board. We realized that, and we did it."

Having Wright, with the speed of an Olympic sprinter, helped. "There aren't many people in the conference or the country who can cover Alexander Wright," Slack said. "We wanted to get the ball to him downfield." When it came time to put it away, the Tigers turned to Danley, who left defenders scattered in his

Stacy Danley fights for
yardage.

wake in leading the way to the game-clinching field goal. "Never, ever, ever have I experienced anything like that," Danley says. "I've been to a couple of Super Bowls, but that was an unbelievable experience. Usually, after the first lick, the crowd is out of it as far as you are concerned as a player. You are concentrating on what's going on on the field. That game, it took me about a quarter just to calm down. It was so loud and so emotional."

After winning two straight SEC championships, big things were expected of Auburn in 1989. The Tigers routed Pacific 55–0 in the opener and beat Southern Mississippi 24–3 in the second game to climb to number four in the polls. But on a rainy day in Knoxville, they lost 21–14 to Tennessee in a game that was more lopsided than the score indicated. They got out of Kentucky with a lackluster 24–12 victory and came from behind to beat LSU 10–6. A week later, they lost 22–14 at Florida State and fell to number sixteen in the polls.

The running game, the staple of Auburn offense under Dye, was struggling. When Mississippi State came to town on October 28, Dye vowed that the Tigers would run. The result was a 14–0 victory. A week later, it seemed a third loss was at hand. Florida led 7–3 late, but in the final seconds, Slack hit Shayne Wasden for 25 yards and the winning touchdown on fourth-and-twelve. Auburn would be dominant from that day on.

Louisiana Tech went down 38–23, and ancient foe Georgia was beaten 20–3 to set the stage for Alabama's first visit ever to Jordan-Hare Stadium. "After we lost those two games, a lot of people counted us out," Slack said after the game, "but now we have a share of the SEC championship. Things came together for us in the Georgia game. We played great that game, and there was no question in our minds we were going to play great today."

Whitt says it was a team that had to grow as the season went along. "We were not as good as people might have thought we were going to be at the beginning," Whitt says. "The expectations were high, but those expectations came after we'd lost guys like Tracy Rocker, Ron Stallworth, Benji Roland, and Lawyer Tillman. Everybody kept panicking, saying Alabama was coming here and they were going to beat us. When Alabama came in undefeated, everybody had questions. Coach Dye did an unbelievable job of getting the team ready to play a team that was supposedly better than they were."

In the victory dressing room, Dye wept as he poured out his feelings to his players. "I've watched you wrestle with them angels," he told them. "And I've watched you become men." Talking to reporters minutes later, Dye was still emotional: "It's been the most overwhelming experience I've ever been through. Alabama coming here to play is much bigger than who won the game. I believe the Alabama people who came here today and saw the stadium will want to come back."

Curry, bitterly disappointed, nevertheless praised the conquerors. "I could say the noise beat us, and it was loud out there, as loud as any stadium I've ever played in," Curry said. "But it was those guys in blue jerseys and their coaches that beat us." For Auburn people everywhere, it was more than a victory in a big football game. It was a day of redemption, a day to remember always.

Dye says he began to realize, particularly after he was named athletic director, what moving the game to Auburn would mean, not just to those on the field but to the university and the community. Not even he was ready for the outpouring of emotion that accompanied the game: "I don't think anybody could have anticipated the emotion of people, but I realized what it meant to Auburn University, the future, and the community," Dye says. "I told everybody they ought to buy up all the real estate because as soon as that thing became a reality everything in this town was going to be worth 25 percent more. I was wrong by about 275 percent. It was worth about three times what it was before."

The change also paved the way for ticket priority programs at both schools—Tigers Unlimited and Tide Pride—that have pumped millions of dollars into the athletic departments. "Alabama, during the Coach Bryant era, didn't need to worry about season tickets because they sold out every game," Dye says. "With college athletics like it is today, it became a need at Alabama to raise money other than football tickets. They have been able to parlay the Auburn game, just like we have at Auburn, into a tremendous income for ticket priorities. We sell 75,000 season tickets a year and Alabama is selling 75,000 season tickets a year because people are not going to give up the Auburn-Alabama ticket and lose their priority. Moving it to Auburn has not only had a tremendous economic impact on our program at Auburn, but at Alabama."

In 2000 Alabama moved its home game against Auburn to Bryant-Denny Stadium in Tuscaloosa. Legion Field, where the modern Iron Bowl was born, was but a memory. It had the same dramatic economic impact in Tuscaloosa that it had in Auburn. Dye maintains that "To people in Alabama, it is the Masters, the Super Bowl, the World Series or whatever. There is no bigger event."

Auburn won its share of big games at Jordan-Hare Stadium before, and it has won its share of big games at Jordan-Hare Stadium since. But December 2, 1989, stands alone. It always will.

11 and 0!

Patrick Nix didn't play a lot in 1993. He was a sophomore, the backup quarterback pulling hard on the sideline for fifth-year senior starter Stan White. He knew his time was coming, but he never expected it to come so soon. Nix had great moments as Auburn's starter in 1994 and 1995, but none surpassed what he experienced on November 20, 1993. Even before the Tigers played Alabama, they had defied the odds. In Terry Bowden's first season as head coach, in the first year of serious NCAA sanctions, they had won their first ten games. If they could beat Alabama, the defending national champion, they would finish off a story so remarkable that it seemed to be the stuff of fiction.

Nix was not expected to play against Alabama. It was the last game for White, a four-year starter who had become Auburn's all-time leader in passing yards and completions. But White went down with a knee injury midway through the third quarter, ending his college career. It was fourth-and-fifteen at the Alabama 35 when Nix was summoned to go into the game. Alabama led 14–5.

The play call from the sideline was surprising even to Nix, who trotted on to the field feeling no fear, only excitement. With no warm up, Nix was told to throw deep for wide receiver Frank Sanders. It would be a play that would turn the game and earn a place in Auburn football lore. It will forever be known only as "Nix to Sanders." Nix threw for Sanders near the end zone. Sanders, coming back for the ball, grabbed it and dived across the goal line. Alabama still led 14–12 after Scott Etheridge's extra point, but the game had turned.

A 26-yard Etheridge field goal and a 70-yard James Bostic sprint provided the winning points, but it was Nix's pass to Sanders that put Alabama on its heels. For Nix, the son of an Alabama high school coach and a lifelong Auburn fan, it was more than the biggest play in the biggest game of a perfect season. It was a play for which he had waited a lifetime. "I'm still in awe," says Nix, now offensive coordinator at Georgia Tech. "I remember standing in the old interview trailer that Saturday afternoon and thinking 'some kid is in his backyard playing Nix to Sanders right now.' It was a fairy tale. It still is. It's amazing."

The scoreboard says it all at the end of the Auburn-Alabama game in 1993.

Nix knew from a young age what Auburn-Alabama was all about. He wore his colors proudly and stood his ground, fighting if necessary, when his schoolmates ridiculed him. "When I was in the fourth grade in Haleyville, the Friday before the Auburn-Alabama game everybody wore the colors of one school or the other," Nix recollects. "We were probably outnumbered 10–1. I fought anyway. That was when Coach Bryant was at Alabama and Auburn was always the underdog. We were looked down on. I did what I did for all those kids in the fourth grade getting abused."

Nix would throw a touchdown pass the next season to beat number-one Florida in the Swamp. He would lead Auburn to seventeen victories as a starter. But for a kid whose dream was to wear that blue jersey, to play against Alabama, November 20, 1993, was the best. "I remember Bo over the top, breaking the losing streak, the whole thing," Nix says. "When Van Tiffin kicked that field goal for Alabama (in 1985) I almost jumped over the couch trying to block it myself. Based on my ability, I never should have even played at Auburn. I'm a coach now and I don't know if I would sign myself. A lot of quarterbacks have done a lot of things at Auburn, but I was blessed."

On the sideline, Bowden called the play, figuring it would be no worse than a punt if it didn't work. And in his heart, he didn't expect it to work. "We figured it was too far to try a field goal," Bowden remembers. "If it was incomplete, we still had pretty good field position. If it was intercepted, they'd be at their own 5." Sanders had lined up to the wide side all day. Alabama All-American Antonio Langham had shadowed his every move. Because they didn't think Nix could throw it to the end zone to the wide side, Bowden and his brother, Tommy, in the press box decided Sanders should go to the boundary. Langham didn't go with Sanders. "Langham started to go to the boundary, but he and Tommy Johnson waved each other off," Bowden recalls. "It was just enough that Frank could out jump him and catch the ball."

Though it was a team that sent players streaming to the NFL, Bowden says the 1993 Tigers didn't win because of superior talent. They won, he says, because they bought into a new coach and gained confidence with each passing week. "We weren't comparable, talent-wise, to a lot of Auburn teams of the 1980s, but it was a team that was talented enough," Bowden says. "More importantly, it was a team that wanted to win. Most of those guys had signed when Auburn was very successful. They had so much urgency to win. They wanted to win so badly they were willing to buy into anything."

It wasn't just the glamour players who made it happen. Ace Atkins, the son of the fullback on Auburn's 1957 national championship team, was a seldom-used defensive end who came out of nowhere to have two crucial sacks against Florida. Reserve defensive back Mark Johnson intercepted a pass in the end zone to lock up a win over Georgia. "We could hardly play Ace Atkins because he wasn't talented enough," Bowden says. "He has two sacks in the game and gets on the cover of *Sports Illustrated*. Mark Johnson was an improbable hero. The 1993 season was about improbable heroes, about a lot of people who had potential but had never come close to reaching it before."

After dominating the Southeastern Conference for most of the 1980s, Auburn had hit on hard times in 1993. Former defensive back Eric Ramsey had gone public with tape recordings that implicated an Auburn assistant coach. The Tigers staggered to a 5–6 record in 1991 and a 5–5–1 record in 1992. With NCAA sanctions looming, Pat Dye, who had built a powerhouse, resigned at the end of the 1992 season.

Bowden, the thirty-seven-year-old coach at Samford University in Birmingham and the son of famed Florida State coach Bobby Bowden, was the surprise choice to be head coach. He was introduced on December 18, 1992. Months later, the NCAA hit Auburn with stiff sanctions. The 1993 team would not be able to go to a bowl game or play on television. As the season neared, Bowden had plenty of questions. He didn't have many answers. Would the system he'd used successfully at Division I-AA Samford work at Auburn? Did he have enough talent to win against a brutal SEC schedule? Would Auburn players be able to push through the disappointment of NCAA sanctions that took away the possibility of postseason play, television, and an SEC championship? If those things fell into place, Bowden thought, maybe he could win six games and have a winning record in his first season as Auburn's head coach. Privately, he later said, he thought even winning six games would be a long shot.

Things fell into place, all right. They fell into place so well that Bowden made coaching history, and the 1993 Tigers made school history. Bowden became the first head coach to go 11–0 in his first season in Division I-A and was national Coach of the Year. Auburn got its first 11–0 season and its first perfect season since the 1957 national champions went 10–0.

Bowden's imaginative ways, combined with the hard-nosed mentality left behind by Dye, developed into a potent offense as the season went on. Though no one knew it at the time, the 1993 team was one of the more talented ever to play at Auburn. And the players, who had suffered through two nonwinning seasons and two years of controversy over Ramsey's allegations of illegal payments, were hungry for better times.

Bowden rebuilt programs at Salem College and Samford. Well into the 1993 season, he thought he was in a rebuilding mode. "I had gone to Salem, a team that was terrible, and lost the last seven games my first year," notes Bowden, now an analyst for ABC. "We won the conference the next year. When I went to Samford and we moved up from Division III to I-AA, it was 4–7 and 5–6. I just assumed there would be the same progression at Auburn."

Bowden had grown up around major college football, but most of his coaching days had been spent in the minor leagues.

When he arrived at Auburn, his first chore was to convince his players that he could win. He also had to convince himself. "I meet with the players, and you don't see a lot of confidence in their eyes. I'm thinking to myself 'If I can get six wins, that will be a step up.' You don't see a lot that suggests you can get more than six wins. You try to motivate the kids to do that, to go out and be better than they were before." Less than a year later, Bowden was celebrating wildly on the turf at Jordan-Hare Stadium, hugging Dye and anyone else in sight. Auburn had beaten Alabama to finish off its perfect season.

Dynamics were at work that even Bowden couldn't see. First, there was much more talent than he or anyone else imagined: Offensive linemen Wayne Gandy, Anthony Redmon, and Willie Anderson; tailbacks James Bostic and Stephen Davis; fullback Tony Richardson; wide receiver Frank Sanders; linebacker Anthony Harris; defensive backs Calvin Jackson and Chris Shelling; defensive ends Willie Whitehead and Gary Walker; and quarterback Stan White all went on to play in the NFL. Shannon Roubique would be a three-time All-SEC center and Andy Fuller would be one of the SEC's top tight ends. Defensive back Brian Robinson would become an All-American.

The pipeline that Dye had started from Dillard High School in Fort Lauderdale began to pay off. Dye had signed Otis Mounds—who had been in jail on a drug conviction—when others backed away. Sanders, Jackson, Robinson, and Bostic soon followed Mounds to Auburn. All made major contributions. Bostic rushed for 1,205 yards on 199 carries in 1993. Sanders caught 48 passes for 842 yards and 6 touchdowns. Robinson intercepted 5 passes.

The Rise and Fall of Terry Bowden

No other coach in the history of Division I-A has ever gone 11–0 in his first season. No other coach in the history of Division I-A has ever won his first twenty games. In 1993 and 1994 Terry Bowden stood alone. The son of famed Florida State coach Bobby Bowden, he was the rising young star among college football coaches. But it wouldn't last.

The Tigers slipped to 8–4 in 1995 and 1996. With spectacular Dameyune Craig at quarterback, they won ten games in 1997 and lost 30–29 to Tennessee in the SEC Championship Game. In 1998 trouble hit. The Tigers lost five of their first six games. Bowden, convinced he would be fired at season's end, resigned amid a storm of controversy. Bill Oliver was named interim head coach. In November 1998 Tommy Tuberville was named head coach, moving from Ole Miss.

"What was probably supposed to happen is I was supposed to get some kind of job and leave Auburn," reflects Bowden. "Most people would have said 'One tough year and you walk out on us.' When I left, although it was controversial, I was able to at least go out on my own terms." Bowden eventually became an analyst for ABC's college football telecasts and remains in that role today.

"I had five and a half years at Auburn, five of them very memorable. It led to a great situation. I went from presenting football as a coach on the sideline to presenting football to the nation from a studio. When people try to find a silver lining, the Auburn experience led me to something that is just as exciting, to be a spokesperson for college football every Saturday. A lot of coaches spend their whole careers hoping they can finish doing well enough to have a job like I have. It's just as exciting as coaching."

Sanders's story was like the story of the 1993 Tigers, as unlikely as it was inspiring. His career almost ended before it got off the ground. Tommy Bowden, Dye's offensive coordinator and wide-receivers coach, had heard and seen all he wanted to see in 1992. He wanted Sanders gone, and the sooner the better. Sanders, then a sophomore, had openly criticized Tommy Bowden's play-calling after a 24–9 loss to Florida. He'd said White should be benched. The week before the Alabama game, he cut loose on Dye. "Had my vote counted, he'd probably have been playing for another team," says Tommy Bowden, now the head coach at Clemson.

The following spring, after Terry Bowden took over as head coach, it seemed Sanders had reached the end of the line. Tommy Bowden didn't think he was giving his best during a scrimmage and told him so. "I walked off the field," says Sanders, who went on to a successful NFL career. "He yelled at me to run and I kept walking." Sanders knew then he was down to his last strike. "It was more than that," says Tommy Bowden. "He'd already swung at his last strike."

But Terry Bowden urged his brother to try to work it out. As maddening as his attitude was, Sanders had talent. Auburn needed him. Tommy Bowden agreed to give it one more try. As Sanders recalls, "He called me into his office. He said, 'This can't work like this. We need you, but we don't need you that bad.'" Sanders, who grew up hard in Fort Lauderdale, decided it was time to change. He became a leader and a star. He helped Auburn win twenty consecutive games. When his career ended, he shared the Auburn record for most receptions with 58 in 1994.

"I matured a lot [at Auburn] as a young man," says Sanders, "probably more than I would have anywhere else in the country.

There are a lot of humble people at Auburn." Sanders earned a degree in psychology and was chosen by the Arizona Cardinals in the second round of the 1995 NFL draft. "Auburn did a lot for me," Sanders says. "I think the way to pay Auburn back is to be the kind of person they try to make their student-athletes be, to be a humble, hard-working American citizen."

Bowden's offense got much of the glory in 1993, but Wayne Hall's defense deserved at least equal billing. Almost unnoticed

Bowden and Dye celebrate the 1993 win over Alabama.

in the unhappiness of the previous season was that Auburn had finished fifth in the nation in total defense. Bowden retained defensive coordinator Hall.

Dye readily admits he probably wouldn't have gone 11–0 had he still been the coach in 1993. But he says he handed Bowden a team that was ready to win again. "We got our mental toughness back in 1992," Dye says. "They were freshmen and sophomores, just babies. You can go down that list and there weren't many highly recruited players. It was kids that came here because of the program."

When Bowden resigned midway through the 1998 season, his tenure coming to a bitter and unhappy end, his relationship with Dye bordered on hostile. But in 1993 they seemed to be best of friends. To this day, Dye maintains, Bowden did "an unbelievable job" that first season. "He basically had a football team ready to play. He didn't do anything to take away from that. They were conservative offensively. He kept Wayne Hall. They were hungry because they'd been through all that stuff."

Auburn had already achieved Bowden's goal of winning six games when Florida came calling on October 16. There had been a 34–10 rout of LSU, but LSU would prove to be not very strong. This would be the test. Few people gave the Tigers much of a chance against the high-scoring Gators. Late in the first quarter, it seemed Auburn didn't have much of a chance. Florida was up 10–0 and driving relentlessly to make it 17–0. But Jackson intercepted a Danny Wuerffel pass and returned it 96 yards for a touchdown. Until "Nix to Sanders," that interception return was probably the biggest play in the 1993 season. "The coaches kept saying we need a big play," Jackson said when it was over. "I just stepped in front of the receiver, made the catch, and saw nothing but green in front of me."

Florida seemed to have taken over again by halftime, leading 27–14. But Auburn wouldn't go away. White hit Richardson with a touchdown pass, Bostic ran for a touchdown. Wuerffel answered every Auburn charge. Finally, with players and fans near emotional exhaustion, Auburn got the ball in the final minutes with the score tied at 35. With 1:21 left in the game, Scott Etheridge kicked a 41-yard field goal and Auburn had done what so many deemed impossible. It had beaten Florida. It was then that Bowden, his players, and people across the nation knew Auburn could win them all. "Florida was better than us and should have beaten us," says Bowden. "When we won that game, it told us that if we play our best, we can beat anybody on our schedule. That was the first indication that this wasn't just a winning team, but a team that could win a bunch."

Joe Whitt had been around greatness before. He'd come to Auburn as an assistant when Dye hired him in 1981. He's still there today, coaching linebackers for Tommy Tuberville. The 1993 season, he observes, was a career moment, one he'll cherish always. "It was a great feeling against all those odds," Whitt says. "Every week it got better. Florida's about to put us away and Calvin Jackson intercepts the ball and runs it for a touchdown. The thing I remember is that in the fourth quarter, we were better than they were. Guys who couldn't get to the quarterback earlier were getting there in the fourth quarter and knocking him down. I thought Coach Bowden came in and pulled the team together in a tough, tough situation. He got them focused and kept them focused as well as anybody could have. I don't think anybody could have done a better job of holding a team together from the time the probation was put on us."

The season didn't start like anything special. Auburn beat an ordinary Ole Miss team 16–12, hanging on for dear life after taking a 16–0 lead. A 35–7 win over Samford didn't excite anybody. Even the rout of LSU didn't convince Bowden. "LSU wasn't very good," he says. "We were able to do some things in our game plan we hadn't done before, and they weren't really ready for it." It took an interception return for a touchdown and a late goal-line stand to win 14–10 at Vanderbilt. So it went until Florida came to town a favorite and went home a loser.

When the season was over, when Alabama had been beaten and Auburn had assured itself of a top-five finish, brothers Terry and Tommy Bowden shared a special moment. Tommy, the oldest, had been the offensive coordinator in Dye's final two seasons. He could not hide his discomfort when his little brother became head coach. "After the Alabama game and all the celebrating, I remember seeing Tommy," the younger Bowden recalls. "He'd had a very difficult experience as coordinator, then being his little brother's assistant. I remember him saying, 'Terry, you just had one of the most unbelievable seasons ever.' Once the game ended, it was a blur. It was a career experience. I've said many times, if I ever get back into coaching, all I could do is experience things again. I don't have the urgency to get back in because I've been fortunate enough to experience days like that one."

Running Back U

The anticipation is rising inside Gadsden Convention Hall. It's almost time for the highlight of a day-long workshop for residents of public housing. "There he is," someone says excitedly. Carnell Williams is walking toward the door. Williams stops to do an interview with a television reporter. Before he can get to the door, he has signed numerous autographs. The man known to all in Gadsden as "Cadillac" has come home.

Williams quickly agreed when he was asked to speak at the workshop. These are his people, especially the young ones. One of Sherry Williams's six children, he lived in public housing as a child. He saw his mother work three jobs to try to make ends meet. He knows their struggles. And he knows what they want most. "My mom was one of those parents who was willing to do anything and everything for us," Williams says. "My sisters had to take care of the house while she worked. That's where I got my work ethic from. I would see my mom work all the time and how she would be tired. I used to always tell her, 'Mama, one day I'm going to build you a house and get you off your feet.' Maybe one day I might have a chance to do that."

For more than an hour, Williams signs autographs. The line is still long when he is called to speak. The room goes quiet. "I know times are tough and I understand the environment you are growing up in," Williams tells the crowd. "Just stay focused. Keep God first and stay focused in life." Soon Williams is sitting again. He signs autographs for another hour, until the line is gone. He poses for photographs with anybody who asks. Williams laughs and says his arm needs a rest. When children are around, Williams is never too busy. "When I was young, I just saw the guys on TV," Williams says. "I was like, 'Man, I wish I could be like them and do that.' I would have loved for one of those guys to come in and talk to me."

At Etowah High School in nearby Attalla, Williams was a hero long before he was an All-American at Auburn. They still talk about the moves he made, the touchdowns he scored. Michael Williams saw it long before that, when his little brother would play with tears in his eyes but never back down.

"[Michael] used to take us out to the park and we played tackle football," Carnell reminisces. "At first, when guys would tackle me, they would just kind of grab me and put me down. He would say 'No, no, no! He's not a little boy. Hit him like anybody else.' I think that's where I got my toughness."

Michael Williams was a promising football player in his own right until he underwent knee surgery in middle school. After that, he concentrated on basketball. "God came along and blessed my little brother and passed it down to him," Michael Williams says. "I get a joy out of seeing him do it. I had him in the backyard knocking him around. He'd get his knee cut and I'd say 'Get up and run.' I molded that toughness, but he has a gift."

Williams was eleven when he played organized football for the first time for the Attalla Roadrunners, and that gift was on display for all to see. "I remember it like it was yesterday," Williams says. "I tried out for the team, made it, and took it from there. I was a running back and wore 24. I think I scored like 40 touchdowns that first year." By his freshman year of high school, Williams was playing on the Etowah varsity, though he had to wait his turn behind Derrick Nix, who would become a star at Southern Mississippi. Raymond Farmer, then the Etowah coach, became a major influence in Williams's life. "It's a blessing that I went to Etowah and was around the kinds of coaches that pushed me as a player," Williams says. "I've talked to other players, and their coaches didn't even make them practice. Coach Farmer treated me like I was Joe Blow." Farmer knew Williams was no Joe Blow. After Williams's freshman year, Farmer called him in for a talk. "He told me he'd never coached a player like me, with my attitude and skills. He said if I continued to work hard and do everything full speed, he felt like I could be one of the best players in the nation. Ever since then, I've just been a worker."

Williams had one of the great careers in Alabama high school history, rushing for more than 6,000 yards. He was an All-American and one of the nation's hottest prospects. But to those who knew him best, he was still the easygoing little boy with the friendly smile, a loyal son, brother, and friend.

Though Williams's parents parted when he was young, his football career has brought his family closer. He has eight brothers and sisters. "We all get along great—his brothers and sisters, his mother, my wife," says Carnell's father, Aaron Turner. "They go places together and do things together. That's pretty much unheard of."

Williams's family is proud of the man more than the athlete. They looked forward to seeing him graduate as much as they looked forward to seeing his name called in the NFL draft. "I've always taught him to be humble in everything you do," Sherry Williams says. Mrs. Williams encouraged her children to be active, but academics came before sports and faith and family came first. "I'm the type parent that, if you don't get your books, you can't play. I'm not going to have an airhead out there running the ball."

As signing day neared in 2001, Williams struggled to decide where he would go to college. He'd grown up an Alabama fan, but others had made more of an impression. In January he visited Tennessee and was overwhelmed. He returned home and told his parents he was going to be a Vol. Though Auburn's coaches were scheduled for an in-home visit, Williams called assistant coach Terry Price, who had recruited him, and gave him the bad news. "Tennessee is the best place for me. I'm through with the process, so don't call me anymore." Price told him he was going to call coach Tommy Tuberville and give him the news. Williams replied, "Tell [him] thank you, but I'm going to Tennessee." Minutes later, Tuberville was on the telephone. Williams finally agreed to the in-home visit but told his parents Tuberville was wasting his time.

Tuberville arrived with most of his coaching staff. Williams, impressed, went to Auburn for a visit the following weekend. He called an unhappy Tennessee coach Phillip Fulmer and told him he was wavering. He visited Alabama. In the end Auburn was his choice. Williams was lost for the season with a broken collarbone against Alabama just as he seemed to be coming into his own as a freshman. He went down again in the seventh game at Florida as a sophomore. Finally, as a junior, he stayed healthy, rushing for 1,307 yards and 17 touchdowns.

He had another decision to make. He could go to the NFL and become wealthy overnight or stay for another year at Auburn and get his degree. Sherry Williams didn't hesitate to offer her opinion. She told him he'd always finished what he started and that he had an opportunity to be an example for others by finishing his education. "My belief is [that] if it is there for you, it's going to happen," Mrs. Williams says. "What God has for you, nobody can take away." Carnell's father was a minister at Original Grace Church in Ashville, Alabama. He told his son to rely on his instincts and his faith and to do what felt right in his heart. "My father always taught me that every man has to go his own way and make his own decisions," Turner says.

Williams and Ronnie Brown, his friend and running mate, decided the NFL could wait for a year. They made their decisions separately, but they announced them together. Brown, who

Auburn's 1,000-yard Club

Here's a list of Auburn running backs who have racked up more than 1,000 yards rushing in a single season, in descending order by total yards rushing:

Bo Jackson	278 for 1,786	1985
Rudi Johnson	324 for 1,567	2000
Brent Fullwood	167 for 1,391	1986
James Brooks	261 for 1,314	1980
Carnell Williams	241 for 1,307	2003
Stephen Davis	221 for 1,263	1994
Bo Jackson	148 for 1,213	1983
James Brooks	162 for 1,208	1979
Joe Cribs	253 for 1,205	1978
James Bostic	199 for 1,205	1993
Carnell Williams	239 for 1,165	2004
Joe Cribbs	200 for 1,120	1979
Stephen Davis	180 for 1,068	1995
Ronnie Brown	175 for 1,006	2002
Jimmy Sidle	185 for 1,004	1963
Monk Gafford	132 for 1,004	1942

arrived at Auburn in 1999, knew Williams had come in 2000 to take the job he himself wanted. But he reached out to Williams anyway. A friendship that goes beyond football was born. "With all the hype, I thought guys were going to be kind of jealous and not show me things," Williams says. "[Ronnie] took me under his wing. He told me how I had to get through."

Williams and Brown made their last season one for a lifetime. Williams rushed for 1,165 yards and scored 12 touchdowns. He finished his career with 3,831 yards and 36 touchdowns, both second only to 1985 Heisman Trophy winner Bo Jackson. Brown rushed for 913 yards and 8 touchdowns as a senior and finished with 2,707 yards in his career, number six all-time at Auburn. Together, they helped Auburn to the first 13–0 season in school history in 2003. And they put their names on the hallowed list of running backs who found greatness at Auburn.

Jackson, who rushed for 4,303 yards and scored 43 touchdowns in his career, stands alone. But the line behind him is long and distinguished, so much so that twenty-first-century teenagers still see Auburn as a place where runners become heroes.

The following running backs earned their distinguished reputations through sweat, blood, and accomplishment when it mattered most:

Bo Jackson

Vincent "Bo" Jackson will tell you today that had it not been for sports, he would have ended up in reform school. He chose Auburn over Alabama, his childhood favorite, and over the $250,000 signing bonus the New York Yankees offered him to play baseball. Jackson burst onto the scene as a freshman in 1982, Pat Dye's second season as Auburn head coach. He led the way to Dye's first SEC championship in 1983. In 1985 he won the Heisman Trophy, edging Iowa quarterback Chuck Long.

Running back James Brooks

Jackson went on to become perhaps the most famous two-sport athlete in history, making the Pro Bowl as a running back with the Oakland Raiders and the major league All-Star game as an outfielder with the Kansas City Royals and Chicago White Sox. He is a member of the Alabama Sports Hall of Fame and College Football Hall of Fame.

James Brooks

Brooks arrived at Auburn from Warner Robbins, Georgia, in 1977, a time when Auburn football was at a low ebb. Shug Jordan had retired and had been replaced by Doug Barfield. The talent level had dropped dramatically. Brooks never made Auburn a big winner, but he made himself one of the more feared backs in America. He rushed for 3,523 yards and 24 touchdowns on his way to an all-star career in the NFL.

Joe Cribbs

Cribbs arrived a year before Brooks, but with much less fanfare. He grew up in Sulligent, Alabama, a short drive from the University of Alabama campus. The Crimson Tide wasn't interested, and that was a mistake. Cribbs rushed for 3,368 yards on 657 carries. His 34 career touchdowns trails only Jackson and Williams. He is a member of the Alabama Sports Hall of Fame.

William Andrews

Andrews doesn't have gaudy numbers. That's partly because he was plagued with injuries early in his career, but mostly it's

Joe Cribbs had 34 career touchdowns for Auburn to his credit.

because he was one of the top blocking fullbacks in SEC history. He rushed 267 times for 1,347 yards and averaged 5.04 yards per carry. From Thomasville, Georga, Andrews went on to become an All-Pro running back with the Atlanta Falcons.

Brent Fullwood

For three years Fullwood was overshadowed by Jackson. In 1986, after Jackson had left, Fullwood made a statement of his own. He rushed for 1,391 yards, the third most in Auburn history, and was an All-American as the Tigers went 10–2. Fullwood, from St. Cloud, Florida, finished his career with 2,789 yards, sixth best in Auburn history. He averaged a remarkable 7.15 yards per carry for his career, the best in Auburn history.

Stephen Davis

Davis was considered the nation's top prospect after he finished a spectacular high school career in Spartanburg, South Carolina, in 1991. He signed with Auburn but had to sit out his freshman year because of academic issues. He spent a year as backup to James Bostic, but when his chance came, he was ready. Davis, big and fast, rushed for 1,263 yards in 1994 and finished his career with 2,811 yards, ranking fourth in Auburn history. He is still a star today with the NFL's Carolina Panthers.

Fob James

Growing up just to the east of Auburn in West Point, Georgia, James learned early that Auburn, then officially known as

Governor Fob James

Auburn running backs have won the Heisman Trophy, been All-Americans and All-Southeastern Conference. They have gone on to be NFL stars. But Fob James stands alone. Not only was he elected governor of the state of Alabama, but he served twice—he was elected as a Democrat in 1978 and as a Republican in 1995. General Douglas MacArthur had it right, James says, in his famous, often-quoted statement: "Today on friendly fields of strife are sown the seeds that on other days and other times will bear the fruits of victory."

"I think the word you have to use is *perseverance*," says James. "You learned perseverance. The competitiveness was awfully good training. There was a lot of pressure on us, but we really weren't aware of it. We had a lot of fun. Coach (Shug) Jordan worked you hard, but no one complained. I loved to go to practice and, as far as I can recall, everyone did."

James rushed for 1,913 yards from 1953 to 1955 and was Auburn's all-time leading rusher until Secedrick McIntyre passed his record in 1976. He stands thirteenth today on the all-time list. He was an All-American and is a member of the Alabama Sports Hall of Fame.

Alabama Polytechnic Institute, was a strong family tradition. His father, Fob Sr., had been a standout basketball and baseball player at Auburn. His uncle was a basketball player and former Auburn mayor. Years later, James's own son, Tim, would carry on the family tradition and play fullback at Auburn.

After his sophomore year at West Point High School, James went away to Baylor Military Academy in Chattanooga. He wasn't so sure he wanted to go, but he wasn't given a choice. "My father determined a little discipline was in order," James says with a chuckle. At Baylor, James blossomed into a star halfback. He wasn't big, but he was fast and he was elusive. He almost went to the U.S. Naval Academy in Annapolis. He thought about Georgia Tech. But in the end, family tradition won out. James rushed for 1,913 yards on 317 carries, an average of better than 6 yards per carry.

He was later twice elected governor of the state.

Rudi Johnson

Johnson played just one season at Auburn, but his impact was so significant that he belongs on the list of the Tigers' greatest. Johnson, from Ettrick, Virginia, played two years at Butler County (Kansas) Community College. Auburn coaches were scouting quarterback Daniel Cobb when they got their first glimpse of Johnson.

In 2000 Johnson rushed for 1,567 yards on 324 carries. There were faster backs, but none were tougher or more durable. Johnson didn't just talk about getting stronger as games went on. He did it. With Johnson leading the way, Tommy Tuberville's second Auburn team won nine games and played in the SEC Championship Game. Johnson was named SEC Player of the Year. He left after that season for the NFL and is a star today with the Cincinnati Bengals.

Rudi Johnson was named SEC
Player of the Year in 2000.
Todd Van Emst

Tommie Agee

Agee was a four-year starter at fullback from 1983 through 1986, first in the Wishbone and later in the I-formation. He was a powerful runner and dominating blocker who rushed for 1,735 yards on 356 carries in his career. Agee, who grew up an Alabama fan in Maplesville, Alabama, was one of Dye's early recruits. He went on to an outstanding career with the Seattle Seahawks and Dallas Cowboys in the NFL.

Joe Childress

Childress, from Robertsdale, Alabama, was considered the nation's top fullback his junior and senior seasons. He led the SEC in rushing as a junior in 1954 and was named the SEC Back of the Year. A two-time All-American, Childress went on to be a star with the Chicago Cardinals and the St. Louis Cardinals in the NFL. He is a member of the Alabama Sports Hall of Fame.

Tommy Lorino

Lorino, at 5'7" and 165 pounds, was small even for his time, but he was quick and hard to follow. In the day of two-way players, he was as much a force on defense as on offense. And he was also the punter. Lorino led the SEC in rushing as a sophomore in 1956, gaining 692 yards on just 82 carries. His average of 8.44 yards per rush was an SEC record.

Lorino had a way with championships. He led Bessemer (Alabama) High School to a state championship. He played on

Auburn's first SEC championship baseball team in 1958. And he was a driving force as the Tigers went 10–0 and won the national championship in 1957. He finished his career with 1,486 yards on 227 carries, an average of 6.55 yards per carry.

Terry Henley

Henley was the fast-talking, hard-nosed tailback who epitomized Auburn's 1972 Amazin's. Henley, from Oxford, Alabama, led the SEC with an average of 93.7 yards per game as the Tigers shocked the experts by going 10–1. He was a first-team All-SEC and second-team All-America selection.

Known as "Hee-Haw" by his teammates, Henley carried eleven straight times on Auburn's only touchdown drive in a 10–6 upset of Tennessee. He finished his career with 1,534 yards on 343 carries and is a member of the Alabama Sports Hall of Fame.

Monk Gafford

Gafford is best known for leading Auburn to a 27–13 victory over number-one Georgia in 1942, perhaps the biggest upset in school history. He was an All-American and the SEC Back of the Year that season. Gafford, from Fort Deposit, Alabama, was a decorated hero in World War II. He later played on a U.S. Army team in Europe. General Patton said he was the best back he'd ever seen. Gafford finished his career with 1,373 yards on 43 carries and is a member of the Alabama Sports Hall of Fame.

Team Rushing Records

Most yards in a game: 565 vs. Southwest Louisiana,
September 7, 1985
Most yards in a season: 3,438, 1985
Most attempts in a game: 86 vs. Vanderbilt,
September 29, 1951
Most attempts in a season: 673, 1984
Fewest yards gained in a game: minus-28 vs. Florida,
October 18, 1997
Fewest yards gained in a season: 559, 1947
Highest average per rush in a game: 9.74 vs.
Southwest Louisiana, September 7, 1985
Highest average per rush in a season: 5.66, 1979
Highest yards per game average in a season: 312.5, 1985
Most rushing touchdowns in a game: 8 vs.
UT-Chattanooga, 1995
Most rushing touchdowns in a season: 36, 1985

Tucker Frederickson

Former Auburn coach Shug Jordan called Frederickson the most complete player he ever coached. Frederickson was one of Auburn's all-time great two-way players. He was an overpowering runner and won the Jacobs Trophy as the SEC's best blocker in 1964.

Running back Tucker
Frederickson blasts
through the line.

Frederickson was a star on both sides of the ball and was a consensus All-American as a safety in 1964. The New York Giants made him the first player chosen in the 1965 NFL draft. From Hollywood, Florida, Frederickson is a member of the Alabama Sports Hall of Fame and the College Football Hall of Fame.

James Bostic

Bostic was one of the "Dillard Five," five players who signed with Auburn from Dillard High School in Fort Lauderdale, Florida. Big and fast, Bostic rushed for 1,205 yards on 198 carries, an average of 6.06 yards per carry, helping Auburn to an 11–0 record in 1993. For his career, he rushed for 2,084 yards on 396 carries. He left for the NFL after his junior year, but his career was cut short by injuries.

Uncrowned
Champions

The journey to greatness started in the after-
math of a humbling 26–7 loss at Georgia in
the eleventh game of the 2003 season. That
defeat left the 2003 Auburn football team—
touted as a national championship contender
three months earlier—with a 6–5 record and
a coach taking withering criticism. The goals
of August were all gone when Auburn's seniors had their weekly meeting with coach
Tommy Tuberville on Sunday, November 16.

They made a vow that day to do all they could to finish with a flourish, to leave something for their younger teammates to carry into 2004. All around them controversy swirled. It was common knowledge that Tuberville's job was in jeopardy.

Six days later, the Tigers beat Alabama 28–23, only to learn that forty-eight hours earlier the president, athletic director, and two trustees had sneaked off to meet with Louisville coach Bobby Petrino about replacing Tuberville. After the trip was exposed, Tuberville was given a one-year contract extension and tearfully announced he would remain. The Tigers beat Wisconsin 28–14 in Nashville's Music City Bowl to finish 8–5. The seniors went on their way, and those who remained went to work on preparing for a season of redemption. But not even they could have imagined what was ahead.

Tuberville hired Al Borges as his offensive coordinator in February 2004, and the last piece to the puzzle was in place. Auburn football was about to take off. A year after almost losing his job, Tuberville became the most decorated coach in Auburn history, winning every major Coach of the Year Award.

The Tigers started the 2004 season with easy wins over Louisiana-Monroe and Mississippi State, but a 10–9 victory over defending national champion LSU on September 18 proved to be the turning point in the season of their dreams. They went 11–0 in the regular season, beat Tennessee 38–28 in the Southeastern Conference Championship Game and Virginia Tech 16–13 in the Sugar Bowl for the first 13–0 record in school history.

For those who played and those who coached, it will forever be an article of faith that they should have been at the Orange Bowl, playing in the Bowl Championship Series title game.

Instead, Southern California routed Oklahoma 55–19 and claimed every widely recognized national championship. But Auburn players wear rings that proclaim they were national champions, too. And in their hearts, they will believe it forever. "I don't think anybody can tell me to my face we're not national champions," quarterback Jason Campbell says. "We deserve it. I'll show our ring. I'll show it to USC, Oklahoma. They can show me theirs and I'll show them ours."

Regardless of polls, the 2004 Tigers earned their place in the proud history of Auburn football. They staked a claim as the best ever to wear Auburn blue, maybe even better than the 1957 team that went 10–0 and won the national championship. Eighteen seniors who had been through the good times and the bad were the heart and soul of a team that went to play with purpose and passion Saturday after Saturday.

That senior class was about Campbell who, after being criticized and questioned for three seasons, became the SEC Player of the Year. It was about running backs Carnell Williams and Ronnie Brown, who put the NFL's millions on hold for a year to play for a championship. It was about cornerback Carlos Rogers, who also decided the NFL could wait and won the Jim Thorpe Award as the nation's top defensive back. It was about strong safety Junior Rosegreen, who played the game with ferocity unmatched and became an All-American. It was about Bret Eddins, playing where his father played and becoming one of the SEC's top defensive ends. It was about Jay Ratliff, who was a dominating defensive tackle on the nation's stingiest defense against scoring.

It was also about Jeremy Ingle, the center who came as a walk-on and became the hard-nosed leader on the offensive line.

Carnell Williams had a banner year for the Tigers in 2004.
Todd Van Emst

"This team was so unified," Ingle said. "You don't see that with a lot of teams these days. You see a lot of individuality, people wanting to be superstars. That's really not what this team was about. Jason Campbell was the best player on our team, and he's one of the biggest team guys you'll ever find." Campbell left as the most accurate passer in school history, completing 188 of 270 passes for 2,700 yards and 20 touchdowns as a senior. Williams rushed for 1,165 yards on 239 carries and was an All-American. Brown rushed for 913 yards on 153 carries and joined Williams to form an all-Auburn All-SEC backfield. All were chosen in the first round of the NFL draft, a college football first.

There were plenty of underclassmen, too, who played major roles. Marcus McNeill was an All-America offensive tackle. Travis Williams was considered too small, at 215 pounds, to play middle linebacker. He made All-SEC. So did nose guard Tommy Jackson. Defensive ends Stanley McClover and Quinton Groves were freshman All-Americans. Courtney Taylor became a big-play receiver with few equals.

But it was the seniors who pulled it all together, who wouldn't let their teammates lose sight of where they were going. "You look at Ronnie and Carnell, and you aren't going to find two more unselfish guys in the country," Eddins says. "Either one of those guys would be a first-team All-American by themselves on any team."

For Tuberville, losing those seniors was like losing part of his family. "It was such a special group," Tuberville says. "They worked so hard. The pressure was on them all year long, and they came ready to play in every game. We did not have a bad game, not one. We didn't have a game where we were flat or didn't come to play. You'd like to say every senior class is going to be like that one, but they don't get much better."

After so many games, so many early-morning workouts, those seniors became as close as brothers. "We just kind of know one another on and off the field," Williams said as Auburn prepared to play for its first SEC championship in fifteen years. "We know each other's ability and character. We have played so long together. It seems like forever. That's why this is so special."

That Williams and Brown came back to share the glory at tailback was one of the big stories of 2004, but the biggest story of all was Campbell. Rated one of the nation's top quarterback prospects out of Taylorsville, Mississippi, he had won the job as a redshirt freshman, lost it, won it back, and lost it again. He started thirteen games as a junior but was labeled an underachiever. In the summer of 2004, forty-two candidates were listed in the pre-season for the Davey O'Brien Award, given to the nation's top quarterback. Campbell wasn't one of them.

Campbell, who had a different offensive coordinator and quarterbacks coach every year of his Auburn career, gritted his teeth and pressed on. When the season was over, he was recognized as the best player in the SEC and one of the nation's top quarterbacks. He was the emotional leader of a championship team. "There wasn't a better quarterback in college football," Tuberville says. "He's an unbelievable leader, one of the best I've been around."

It was on the afternoon of September 18 that Campbell emerged as a star and Auburn emerged as a championship contender. The capacity crowd at Jordan-Hare Stadium was in a frenzy. Campbell led Auburn on a last-ditch 59-yard drive, completing a 14-yard pass to Taylor on fourth-and-twelve and a 16-yard touchdown pass to Taylor on third-and-twelve with 1:14 left to tie the score 9–9. Because LSU kicker Ryan Gaudet had missed the extra point after LSU's touchdown, the Tigers could take the lead.

All that remained was for Auburn's John Vaughn to kick the extra point and the comeback would be complete, but the snap from Pete Compton bounced to holder Sam Rives. He got the ball down, but Vaughn's kick was wide. The crowd gasped. But the football gods smiled on the Tigers. LSU's Ronnie Prude, leaping in an attempt to block the kick, came down on Compton's back. The rules say that is a personal foul. Vaughn got another chance. The snap was low again, but Rives got it down again and, this time, Vaughn got it through.

None of it would have happened had it not been for a remarkable play by Williams. With Auburn facing second-and-four at the LSU 33 yard line on the sixth play of the drive, Campbell threw a screen pass for Williams. LSU cornerback Corey Webster read it all the way. He broke on the ball, and for a fleeting moment, had it in his hands. Williams reached in and snatched it away. Six plays later, Campbell threw the deciding pass to Taylor. What might have been a loss became a victory. After that day, the Tigers were overpowering. "We always had confidence, but after that game, our confidence grew so much more," Campbell says. "We believed we could beat anybody we played." And they did.

What would Auburn's offense have been like without Campbell and Taylor or without Williams and Brown at tailback? What would it have been like if McNeill had been sidelined? Where would the defense be without Travis Williams, cornerback Carlos Rogers, or strong safety Junior Rosegreen?

Jason Campbell emerged as one of the nation's best quar-terbacks in his senior year.
Todd Van Emst

The Tigers never had to answer those questions. They stayed remarkably healthy throughout the season, and Tuberville says it wasn't by accident. He gives the credit to strength and conditioning coach Kevin Yoxall and the team's increased depth in key positions. "Players can get hurt any time, but it usually happens when you are tired," Tuberville said. "We had more depth than we've ever had. Players didn't have to play as many snaps. We've been blessed not to have a lot of key injuries."

Even in the bad times, Campbell had faith that everything happens for a reason, but it was difficult sometimes to figure out just what the reason was. Campbell was in and out of the starting lineup for two seasons. Every season brought a new offensive coordinator and quarterbacks coach. Even as he completed a higher percentage of his passes than any quarterback in Auburn history, the criticism grew. He heard boos in his own stadium. "It was like I was playing all twenty-two positions on the football team," Campbell says. But he pressed on, earning the respect of his teammates and coaches. When Borges arrived, he and Campbell quickly bonded. The boos were replaced by cheers.

"People don't realize what he did at the line of scrimmage," Borges says. "He got us out of bad plays, into good plays. He made great decisions. He did a lot of things to win for you other than just with his arm." David Pollack, Georgia's All-America defensive end, thought he saw it watching Auburn on tape. He knew he saw it in the Tigers' 24–6 victory over the Bulldogs. It's that elusive thing called chemistry, and winning without it is next to impossible.

"You can toss a coin as far as talent on most SEC teams," Pollack said. "Everybody has talent. The difference is if you have that chemistry, that love for each other. They have it. You can see it in the way they play together." Auburn players say that this, more than any other factor, is the reason they took a fifteen-game winning streak into the 2005 season.

Rosegreen says he never felt it more than when he intercepted a school-record four passes in Auburn's 34–10 victory at Tennessee. "It was amazing," Rosegreen says. "Everybody was just hugging me and was so excited for me. Nobody was saying 'I wish I got it.' They were happy for me. We love each other like brothers. That will take you a long way." Auburn players had learned hard lessons the year before about dealing with expectations.

The summer of 2003 was a new experience for Auburn's football team. Reporters and photographers from media outlets nationwide swarmed into town. The Tigers had finished the 2002 season with back-to-back wins over top-ten teams. *Sporting News* and the *New York Times* picked them to win the national championship. They were ranked number six in both preseason polls. It was great fun . . . until the season started. USC crashed the party with a 23–0 season-opening victory at Jordan-Hare Stadium. A week later, Georgia Tech pulled a 17–3 stunner in Atlanta. The party was over. As the season neared its end, there wasn't a lot of joy around Auburn's football program.

When Tuberville awoke on the morning of November 22, 2003, in his LaGrange, Georgia, hotel room, he believed the Iron Bowl against Alabama that day at Jordan-Hare Stadium would be his final game as Auburn's football coach.

Tuberville was saddened that he wouldn't be allowed to finish the job he had started when he moved from Ole Miss in November 1998, but he was proud. He was proud of his players and his coaches for their determination and preparation through

Head coach Tommy Tuberville has brought glory back to the Auburn football program.
Todd Van Emst

the swirling controversy of the previous week. On an emotional night, Auburn beat Alabama. Tuberville celebrated with his players for what he and most of those close to the program thought would be the final time.

What Tuberville didn't know was that two days earlier president William Walker, athletic director David Housel, and trustees Earlon McWhorter and Byron Franklin had sneaked away to a small airport near Louisville to talk to Cardinals head coach Bobby Petrino about being Auburn's next coach. Petrino had been Auburn's offensive coordinator in 2002. The trip was exposed days later, sending shock waves through the athletic department and the university as a whole. In the end, Tuberville was left standing. Walker resigned under pressure and Housel retired.

That Auburn's football program emerged stronger than ever, Tuberville says, is a testament to the character and dedication of players and coaches. "I think the most it says is how solid our program is," Tuberville says. "A lot of programs would have fallen apart. Just a little bit of it has to do with me. It's about the assistant coaches and their perseverance through all that, about our players ignoring it and working hard.

"There's no doubt that month made us stronger as a staff, understanding how good this place is and how solid the players on this team are mentally, physically, and spiritually. You can overcome a lot together. If we'd been divided as a football program, we never would have made it."

In the days after the trip was exposed, Tuberville was heartened by thousands of e-mails and letters from Auburn supporters. There was rage at those who made the trip. "I think everybody was disappointed with that season, but we just have a president who didn't understand athletics and didn't understand what building a program is about," Tuberville says. "That wasn't the Auburn people."

Campbell says Auburn players drew strength and resolve from watching how their coach handled the greatest crisis of his professional life. "Everything Coach Tuberville went through meant a lot to that team," Campbell says. "We just rallied around him. The way he showed his composure meant a lot."

Tuberville says it was his players and assistants who made it happen by pulling together. "Our coaches and players did the best job of dealing with the circumstances and winning that game, the best job of focusing I've ever seen," Tuberville says. "The thing we all learned was, no matter what's on the outside, the only thing you can control is what you do."

As the 2004 season approached, things were much quieter. The Tigers were expected to be good, not great. But through the off-season, spring practice, and preseason practice, the belief grew among Auburn players that good things could be ahead. The memory of the disappointment of 2003 drove them in practice, in workouts, in the meeting room. "We learned a lesson," Carnell Williams says. The Tigers vowed they would focus hard on every opponent, every week, and not look ahead or behind. They vowed to take back the respect they believed they had lost. They made a statement against LSU. They made another one with a stunning 34–10 rout of Tennessee in Knoxville. Week after week, it was the same. Most games were decided by halftime.

The biggest statement, perhaps, came on November 13 against number five Georgia. Auburn won 24–6 at Jordan-Hare Stadium, and it could have been worse. Alabama was beaten

Hard-Fighting Soldiers

Locked together, arm-in-arm, they sang loudly, forcefully, sometimes off-key. More than one hundred men, young and old, black and white, swayed back and forth to the words of the song:

I'm a hard fighting soldier on the battlefield,
I'm a hard fighting soldier on the battlefield
I'm a hard fighting soldier on the battlefield
I keep on bringin' souls to Jesus
By the service that I give
I've got a helmet on my head, in my hand a sword
  and shield
I've got a helmet on my head, in my hand a sword
  and shield
I've got a helmet on my head, in my hand a sword
  and shield
I keep on bringin' souls to Jesus
By the service that I give
You gotta walk right, talk right, sing right, pray right,
  on the battlefield.
You gotta walk right, talk right, sing right, pray right,
  on the battlefield.
You gotta walk right, talk right, sing right, pray right,
  on the battlefield.
I keep on bringin' souls to Jesus
By the service that I give
I'm a hard fighting soldier on the battlefield

In that song, Auburn team chaplain Chette Williams says, is the 2004 story of Auburn football. He takes a medallion from his desk that shows a Roman soldier on one side and a scripture on the other. He points out the clip on the soldier's side. "Whenever they were in hostile territory and they saw the enemy coming, they would all hook together," Williams says. "A soldier had to be certain of the person beside him, that he was going to fight. Even if that person got hurt or wounded, the guy hooked up to him had to carry him through."

On the night before Auburn clinched the Southeastern Conference West Division championship at Ole Miss, Williams talked to players about "hooking together." That became a rallying cry for Auburn's football team. And a song came to define a football team.

Defensive end Kyle Derozan, who sang the song "Hard Fighting Soldiers" in his church, introduced it to his teammates at a Fellowship of Christian Athletes meeting. Early in the season, they began to sing it at their Friday night meetings before games. After they beat Ole Miss, they sang it in the locker room.

The public got to see it when locker room footage was shown on coach Tommy Tuberville's weekly television show. "It's amazing," running backs coach Eddie Gran says. "You get in that locker room and you hook up with each other. You have your arms around the guy next to you. It doesn't matter if he's black, white, red or yellow. You sing that song, and you have 140 of us doing that. It's something you'll never forget."

21–13 in Tuscaloosa. Tennessee fell again in the SEC Championship Game. Virginia Tech, winner of eight straight, went down in the Sugar Bowl. That Auburn became the first 13–0 SEC team not to win at least a share of the SEC championship will never be easily accepted. USC and Oklahoma were ranked first and second in the preseason and never lost. That had never happened before.

On the day after the SEC Championship Game, the Tigers got the final word. They would not go to the Orange Bowl to play for the national championship. Campbell spoke eloquently for his teammates. "We are SEC champs, and that's something to be proud of," Campbell said. "It just takes something out of you

Defensive end Stanley McClover in the Sugar Bowl. Todd Van Emst

when you hear commentators say Auburn should just accept it and move on. That's not something you just accept. You work hard, and you think about all the hard work you did to get the opportunity to play in the Orange Bowl. Someone says just accept it. They really don't respect you much as a team.

"We feel like we should be respected. It wasn't something that was given to us. Everyone fought us off. If anyone thinks you are going to play the same team twice, play them in the SEC Championship Game, and walk all over them, they have another think coming. People were talking about Auburn better watch out because Tennessee has an opportunity to upset them. When you win that game, you still don't get respect. You get shot down for not winning convincingly enough."

Campbell said he began to see the likely outcome when Auburn dropped in the BCS standings after beating Alabama. "I feel like we always have to do something extra to push our team to the top," Campbell said. "Every time we play a game, somebody says we have to score so many points. I see some of the other teams struggle and nobody says anything. USC had a battle with UCLA, but people gave us trouble about Alabama. When you are playing a rivalry game, it's all about throwing the records out the window. We tried to tell everyone that, but they don't want to listen."

Tuberville stood up for his team, but as is his way, he kept his composure. "Oh, I've screamed privately," Tuberville said, "but this is the system we chose." Regardless of polls, when it was over, Auburn's football team players knew what they had done. And so did their coach.

Tuberville was part of three national championship teams as an assistant at Miami. The 2004 Tigers, he says, stood alone. The team was honored in December at Toomer's Corner, traditional site of Auburn victory celebrations, and again with a parade after the Sugar Bowl. "I can coach for thirty years or you can watch thirty more years of football and never see a team as close, that plays as well together as this team did," Tuberville said. "We had the most unselfish group of players I've ever been around, and we have the best coaching staff I've been around. I was part of three national championship teams, but this was the best team I've ever been around."

About the Author

Phillip Marshall is currently the beat writer covering the Tigers for the *Huntsville Times*. He has served as sports editor for the *Huntsville News*, the *Decatur Daily*, and the *Montgomery Advertiser*. He is a two-time president of the Alabama Sports Writers Association.

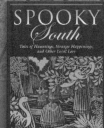
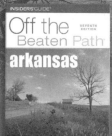

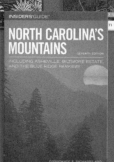